YOU ONLY NEED ONE 'YES'

101 ORIGINAL NEW CARTOONS

SPARE A
FEW BILLION

by Kaamran Hafeez.

AuthorHouse™
1663 Liberty Drive
Bloomington, IN 47403
www.authorhouse.com
Phone: 1 (800) 839-8640

Published by AuthorHouse   03/12/2019

ISBN: 978-1-7283-0323-9 (sc)
ISBN: 978-1-7283-0324-6 (e)

Library of Congress Control Number: 2019902689

Print information available on the last page.

This book is printed on acid-free paper.

authorHOUSE®

Acknowledgements

Special thanks to Sam Gross for his invaluable input. Thank you to Bob Mankoff, Victoria Roberts and Matt Diffee for their generosity. And thank you to Irfaan and Patricia for their encouragement, wealth of ideas and for being two of my biggest fans.

To Mom

For planting the seed.

Foreword

When I was 11 years old, I decided I would be a cartoonist. There was one problem—I didn't know how to come up with ideas. This being the year 19 B.G. (Before Google), I had no way of figuring out on my own how to do that. I concluded that I didn't have what it took and gave it up.

Years later, after finishing a Bachelor of Music, I came across Mischa Richter's tome *The Cartoonist's Muse: A Guide to Generating and Developing Creative Ideas.* It was a revelation! Employing the techniques of association, I was able to generate worthy ideas. It wasn't long before I sold my first cartoon—to King Features' *The New Breed*.

There's a neat little phrase that was very helpful to me when I began my career as a cartoonist: You only need one 'yes'. That applies to both writing and selling cartoons. It doesn't matter how many bad ideas you come up with. If you create one 'good one', you're golden. No matter how many times an editor says 'no', if they say 'yes' once, you're in!

My advice to any aspiring cartoonist with talent: get a day job you can live with, make a commitment to your artistry, and enjoy the ride.

—Kaamran Hafeez
February 2019
Gabriola Island, BC

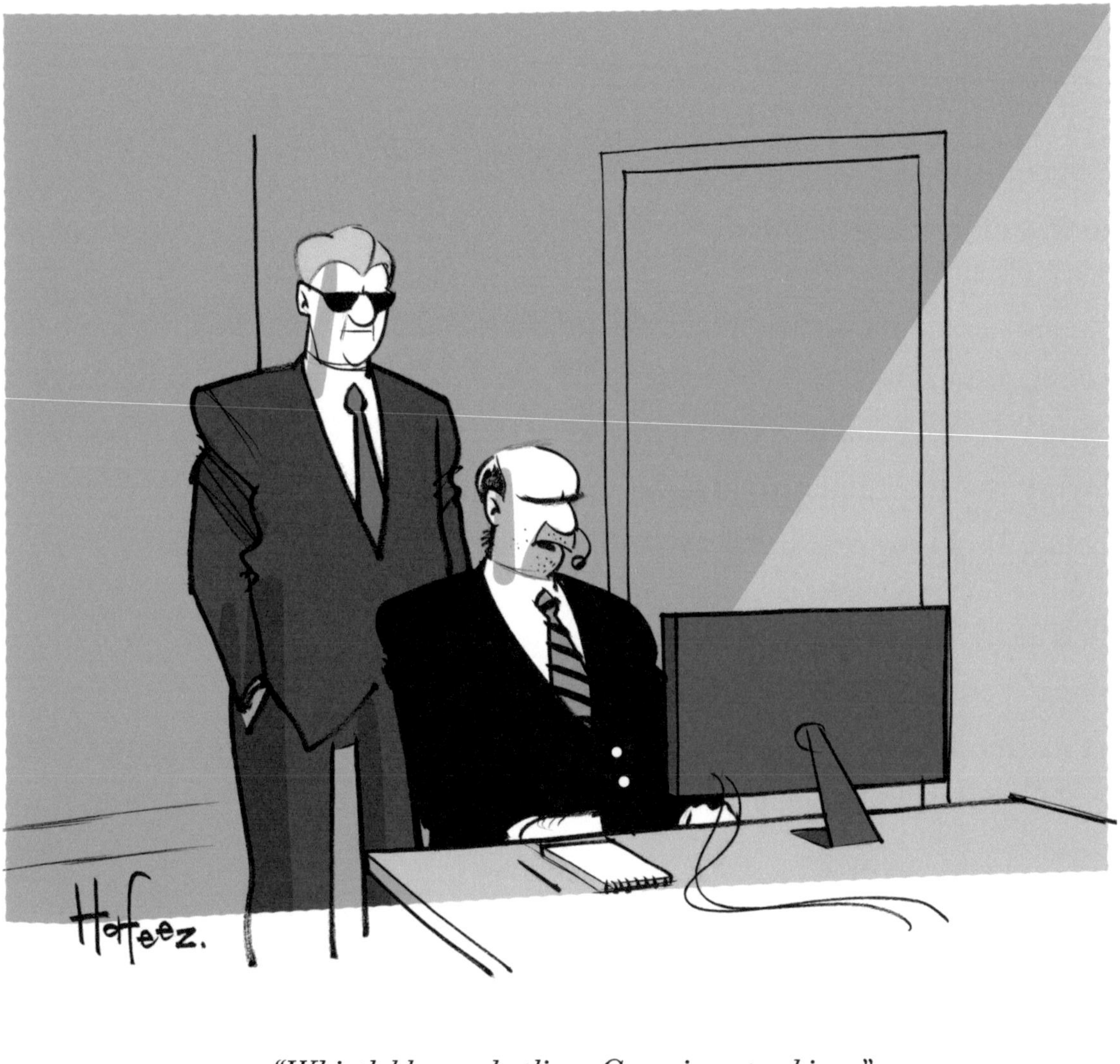
Hafeez.

"Whistleblower hotline, Carmine speaking."

"Butterfield has the flu, Sir—so we're sending him in first."

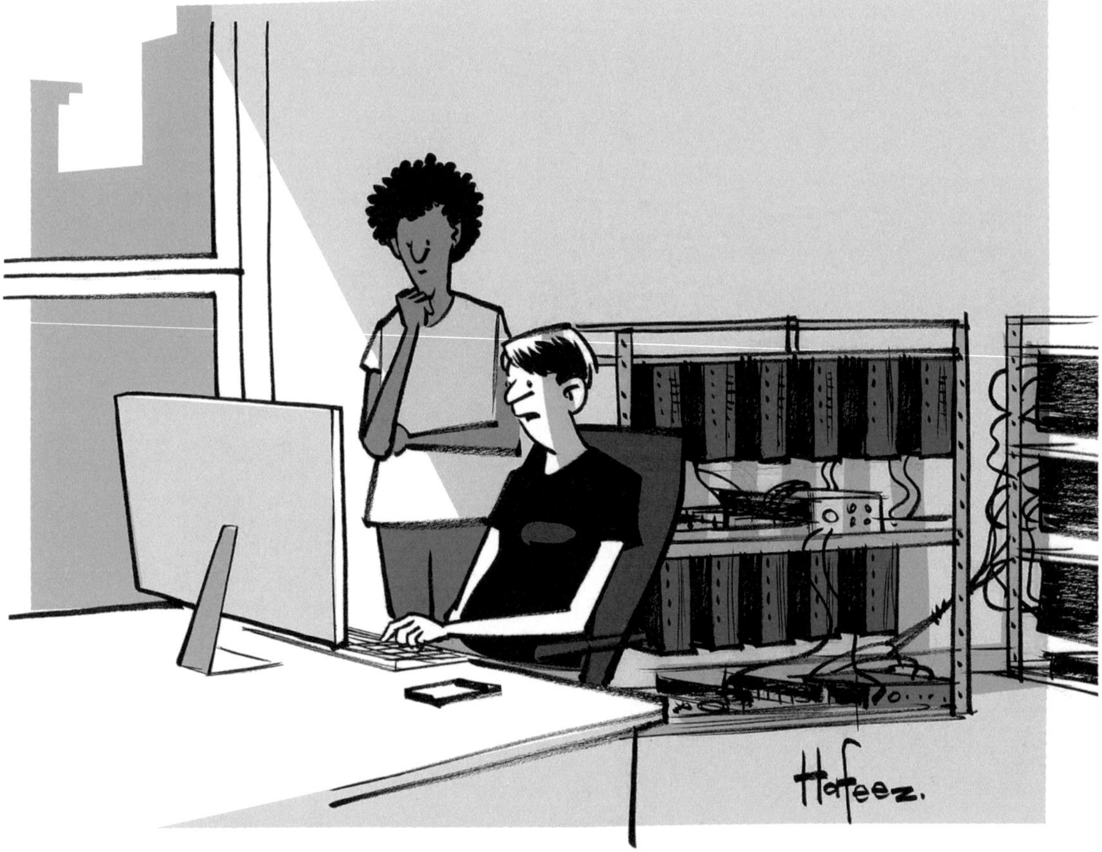
Hafeez.

"We made 3 billion dollars mining Bitcoin, minus our electricity bill—that comes to $1.61"

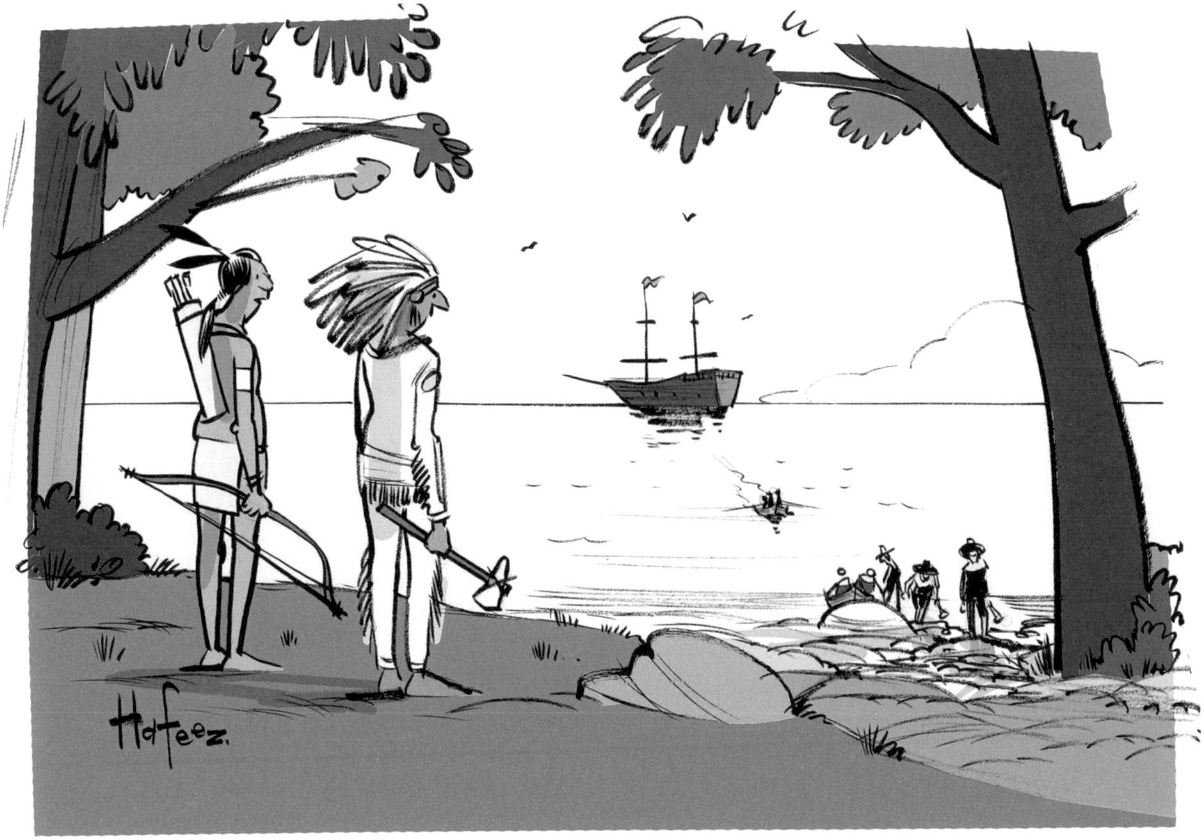
Hafeez.

"The other option is to get them hooked on tobacco."

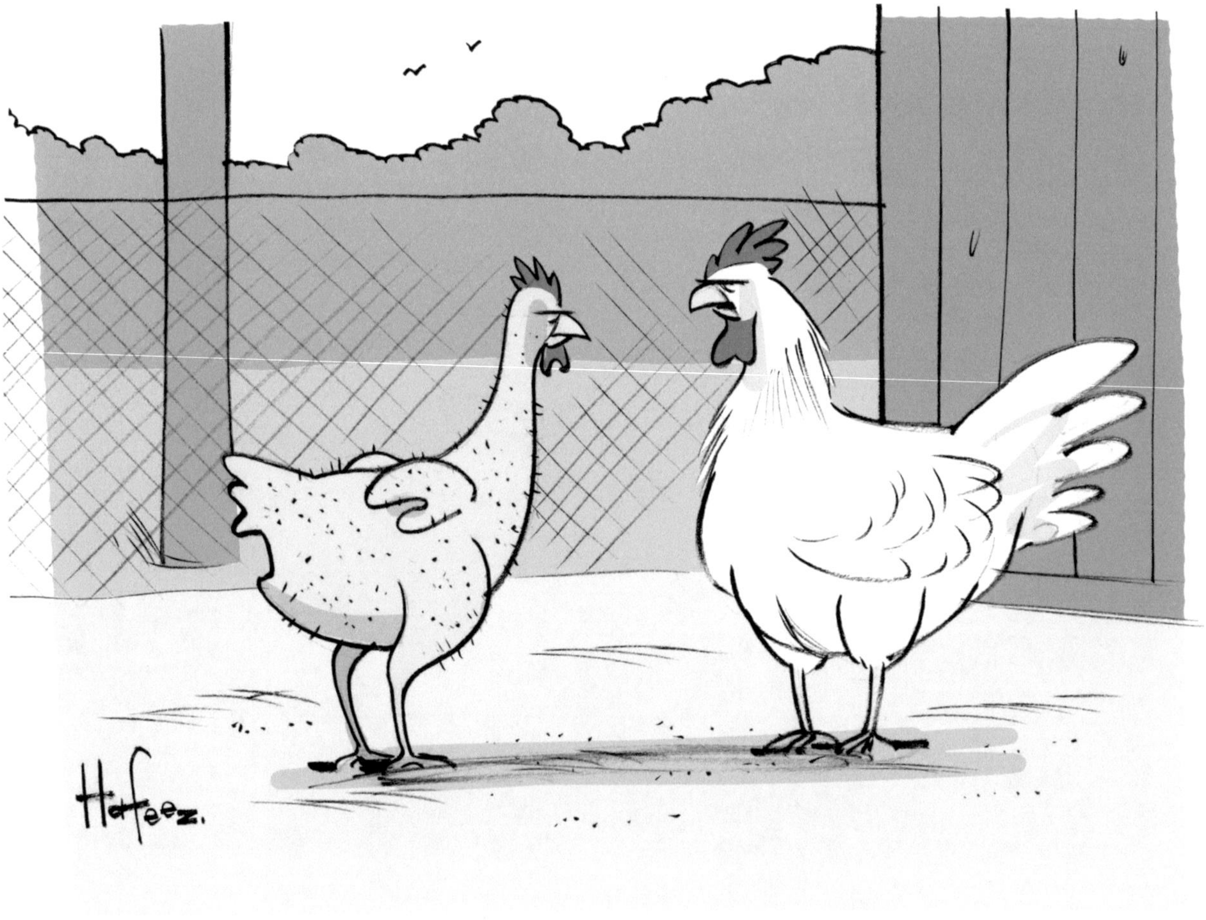
Hafeez.

"Do you write your own material?"

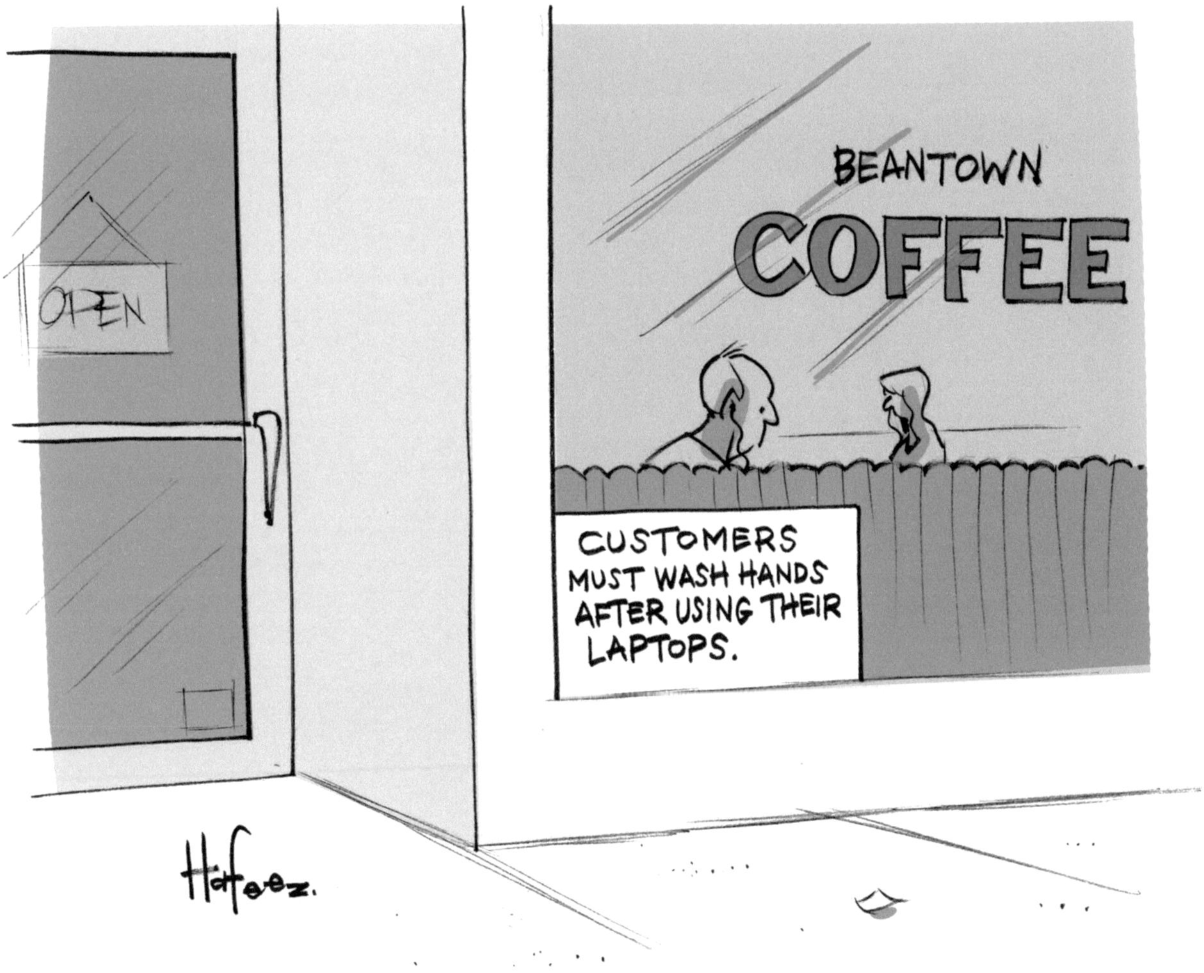
OPEN
BEANTOWN
COFFEE
CUSTOMERS MUST WASH HANDS AFTER USING THEIR LAPTOPS.
Hafeez.

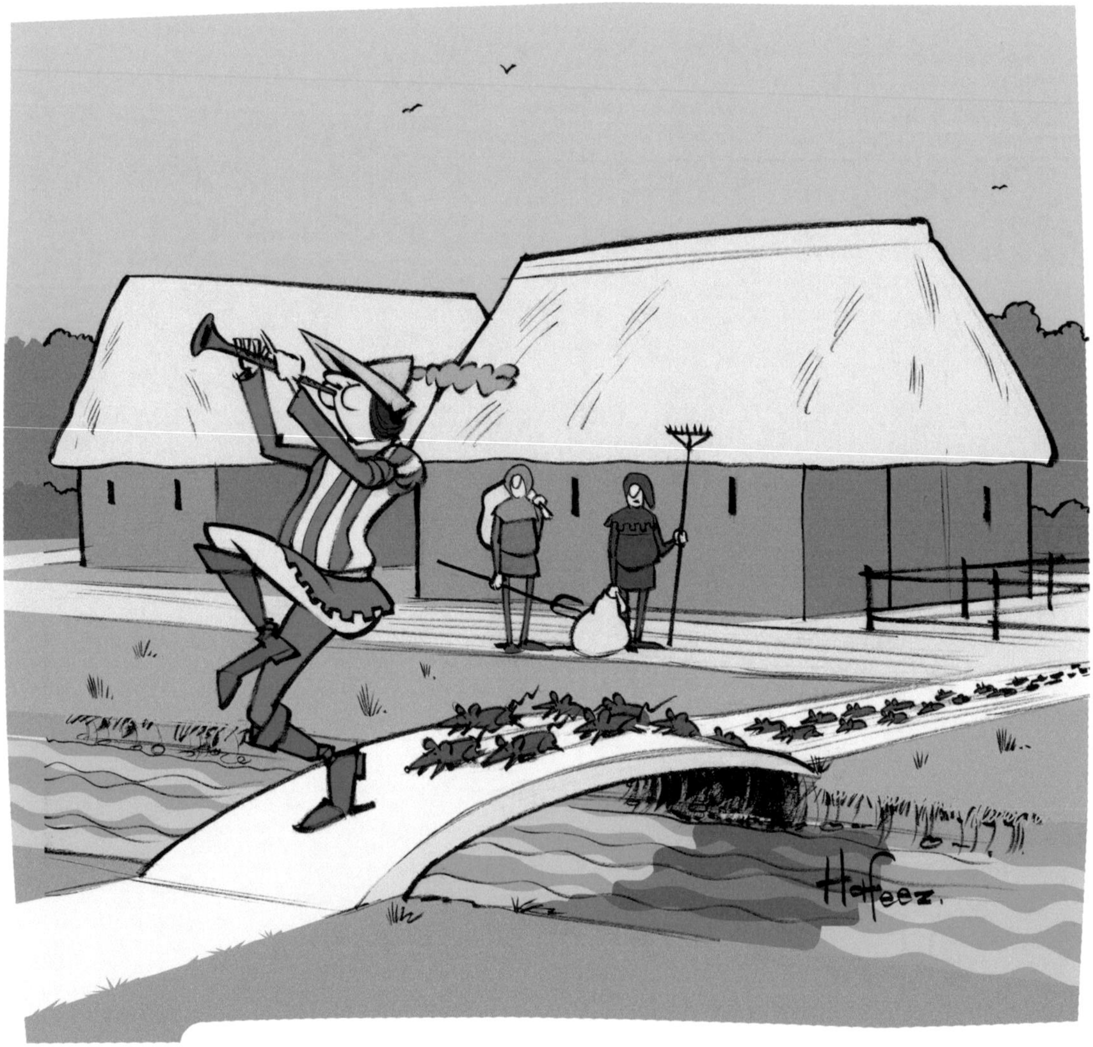
Hafeez.

"I heard he buys all his followers online."

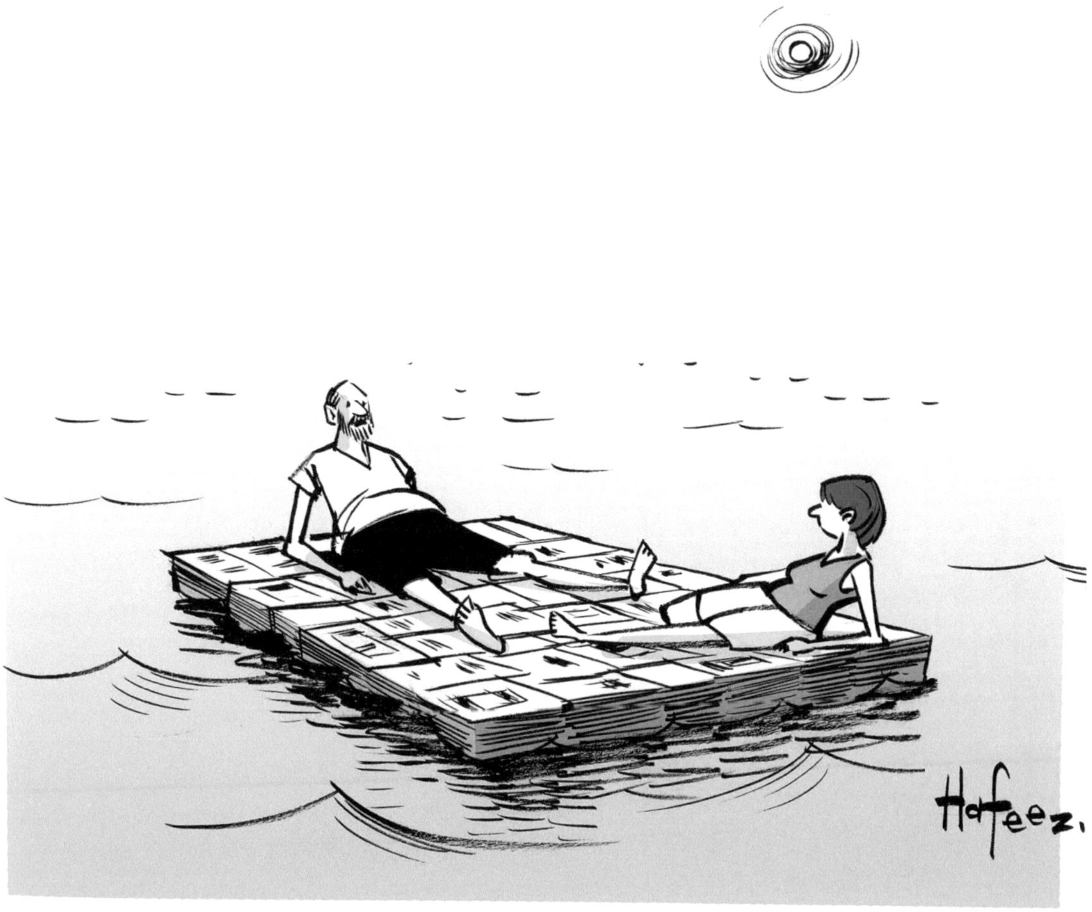
Hafeez.

"I'll bet our creditors are feeling pretty stupid right now for sending us this raft of bills."

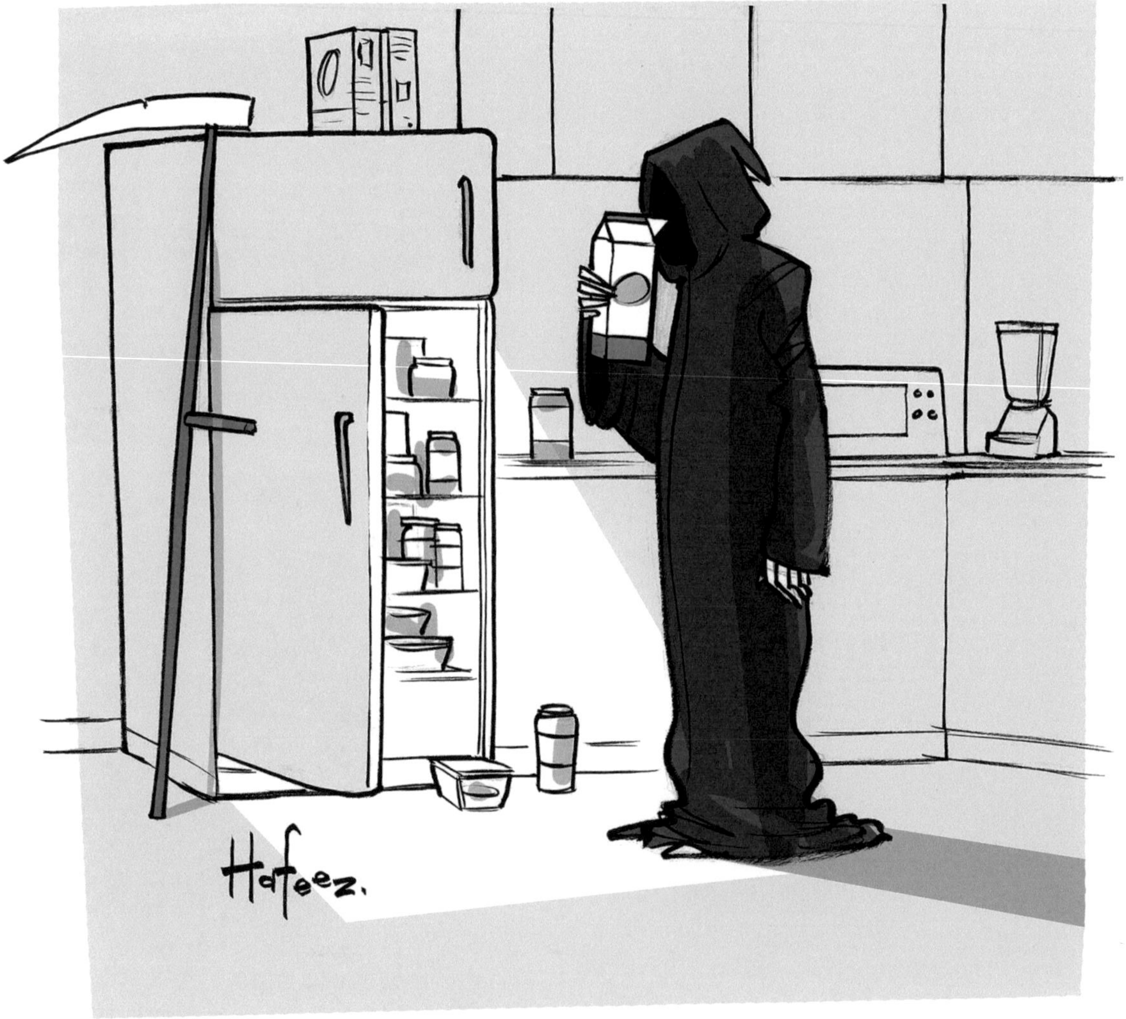
Hafeez.

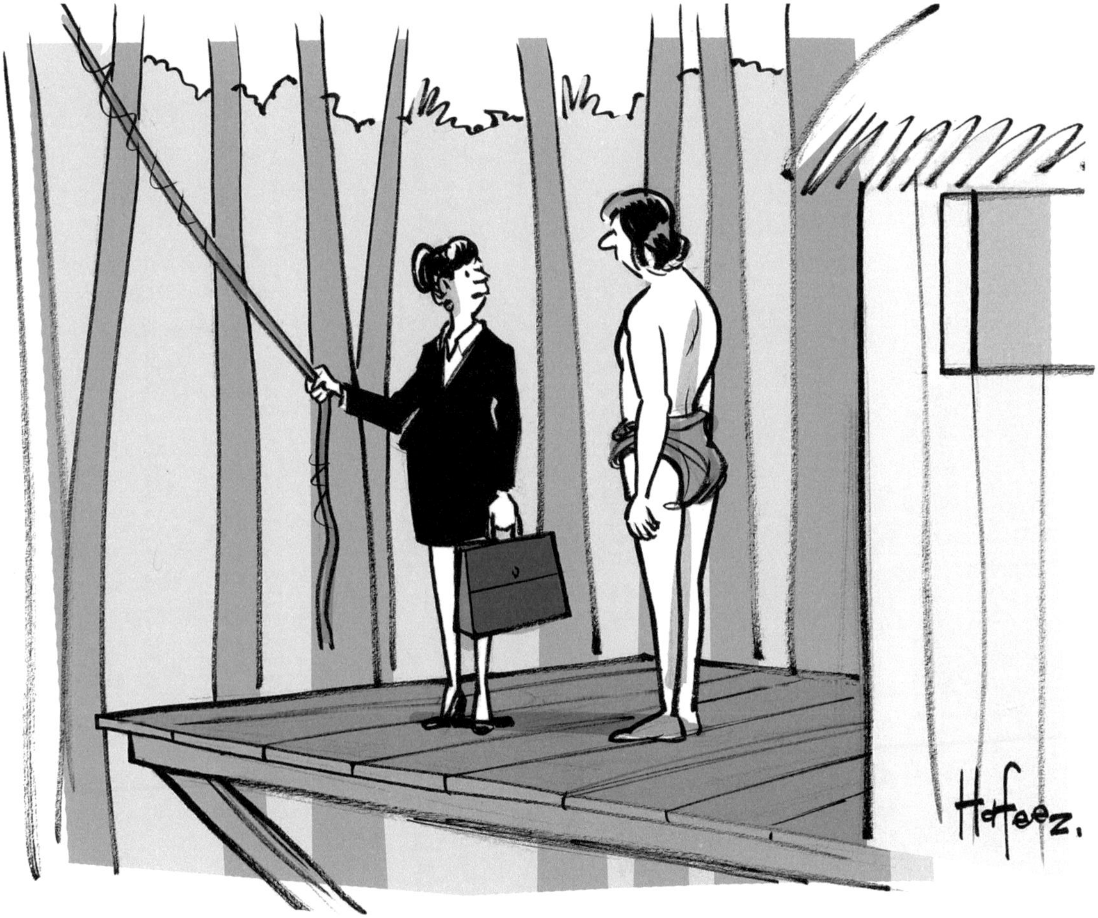
Hafeez.

"Me Tarzan, you Jane."

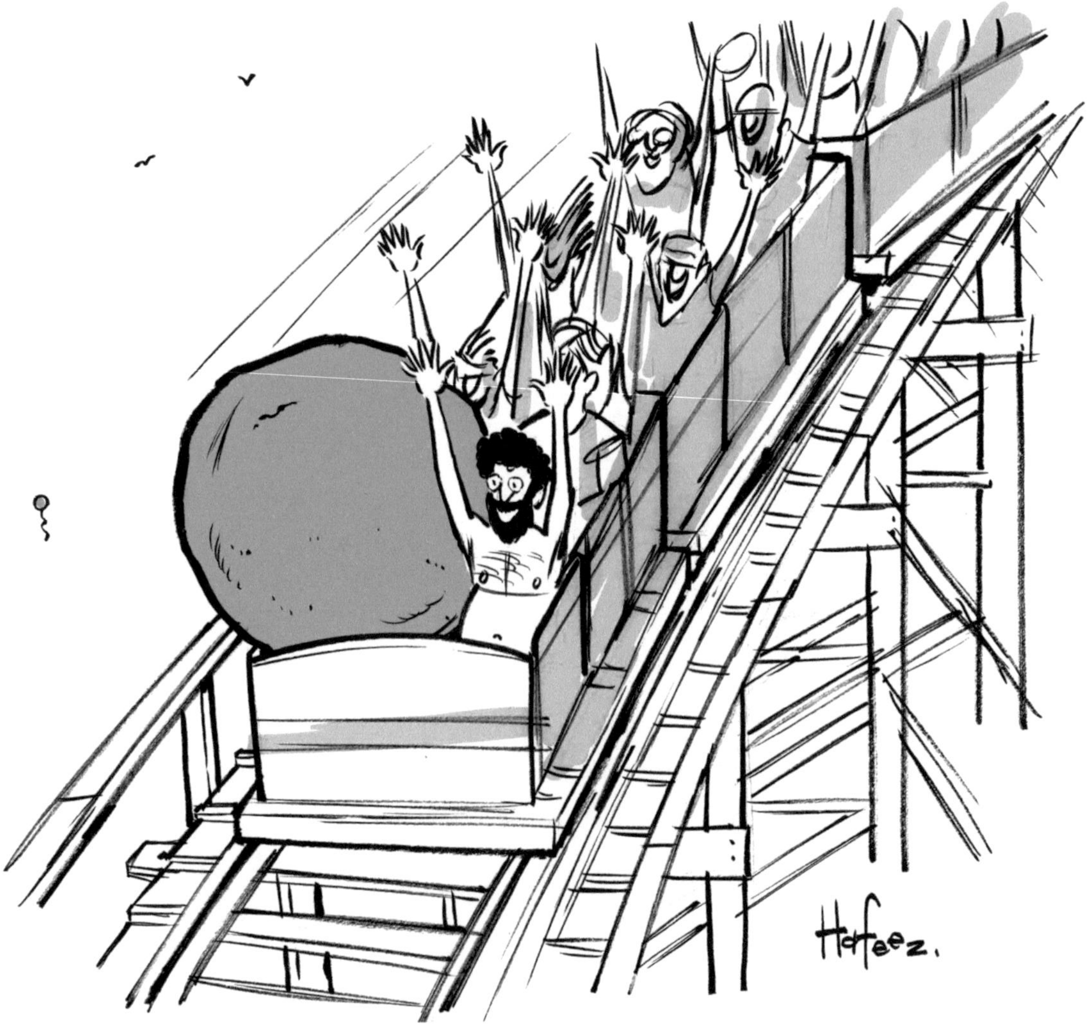
Hafeez.

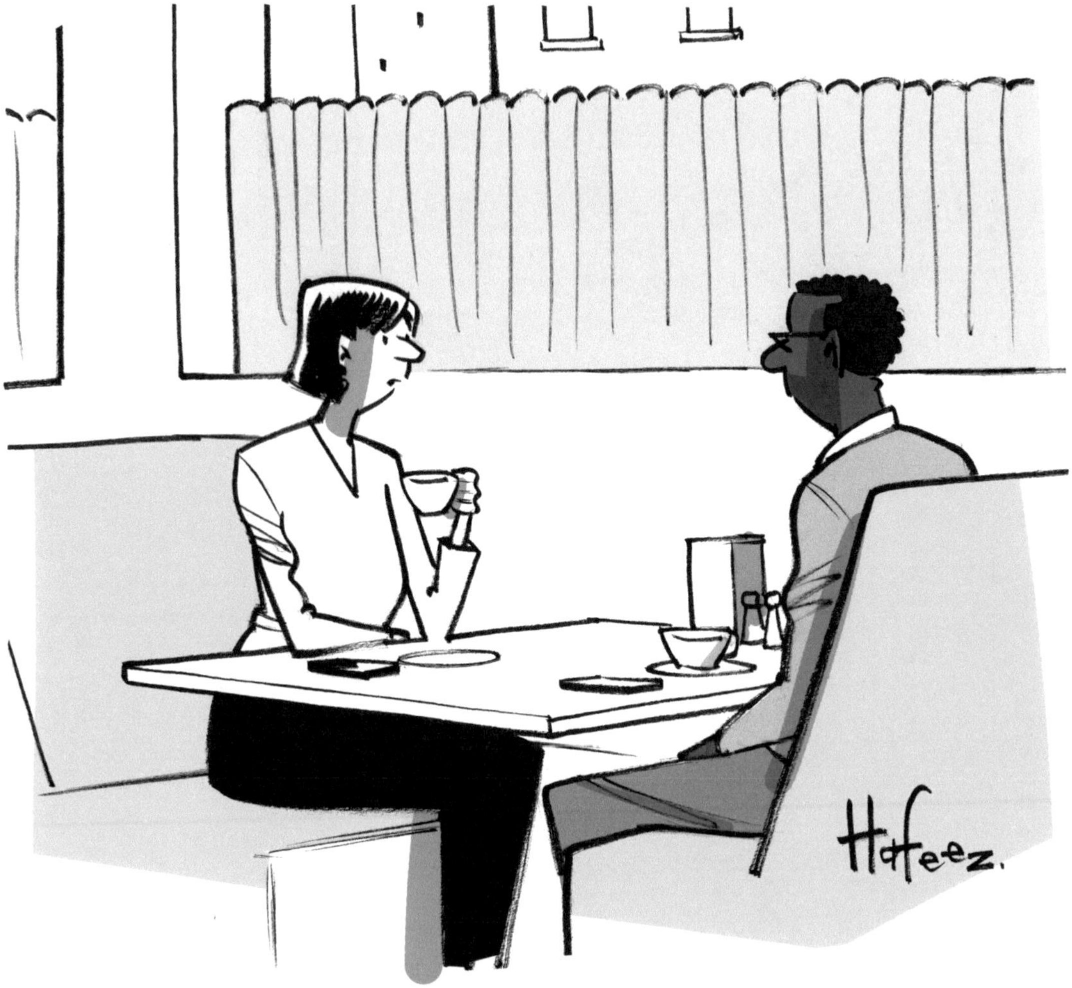
Hafeez.

"I think we should widen the radius on our dating apps."

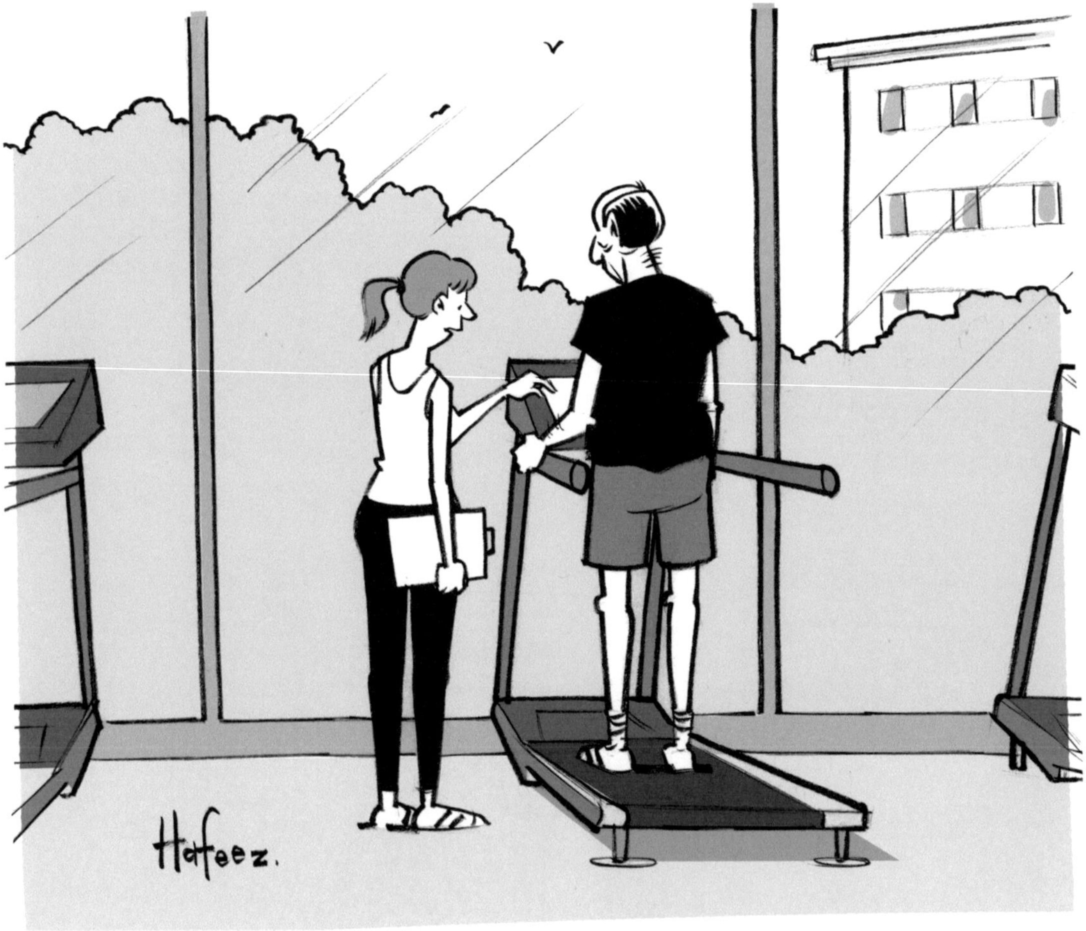
Hafeez.

"... and over here, you can set the level of decline based on your age."

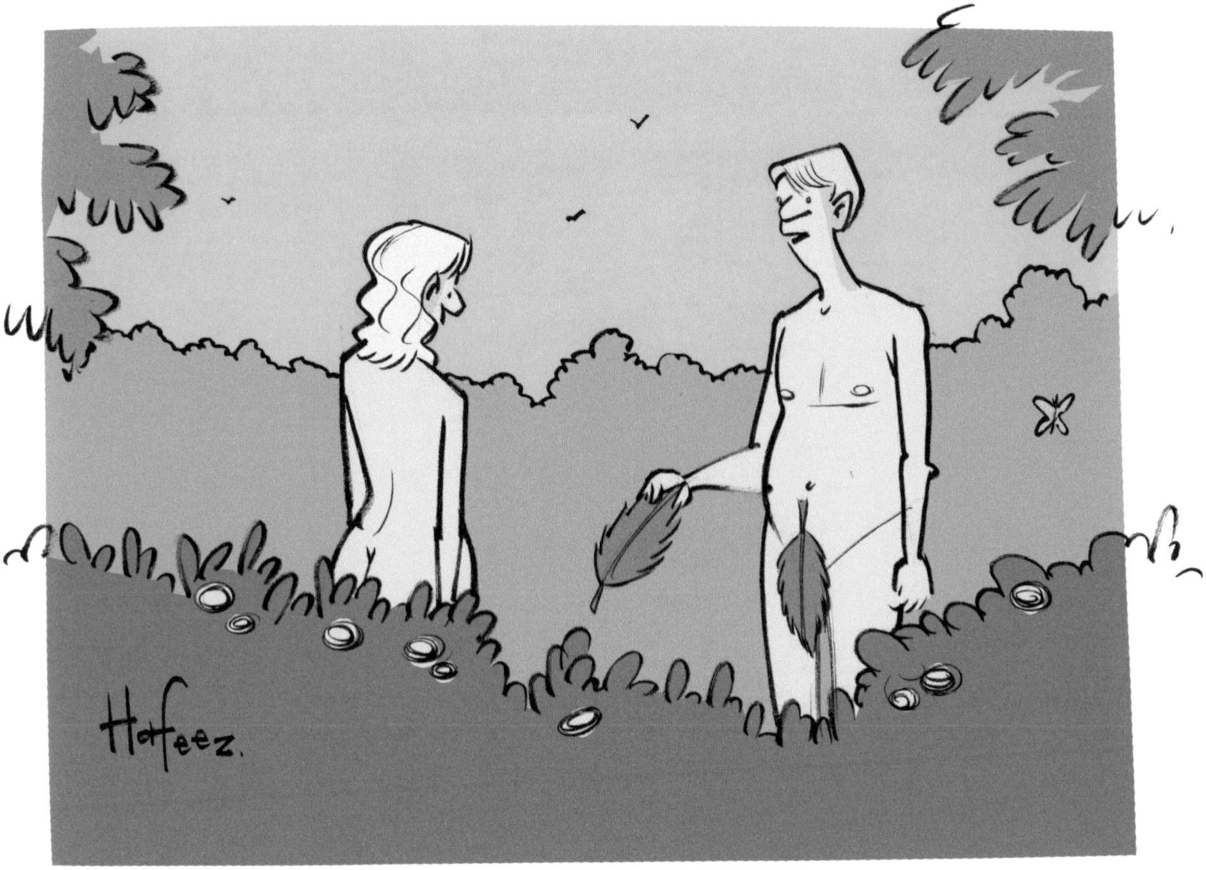
Hafeez.

"I've invented a software application for protecting our personal data."

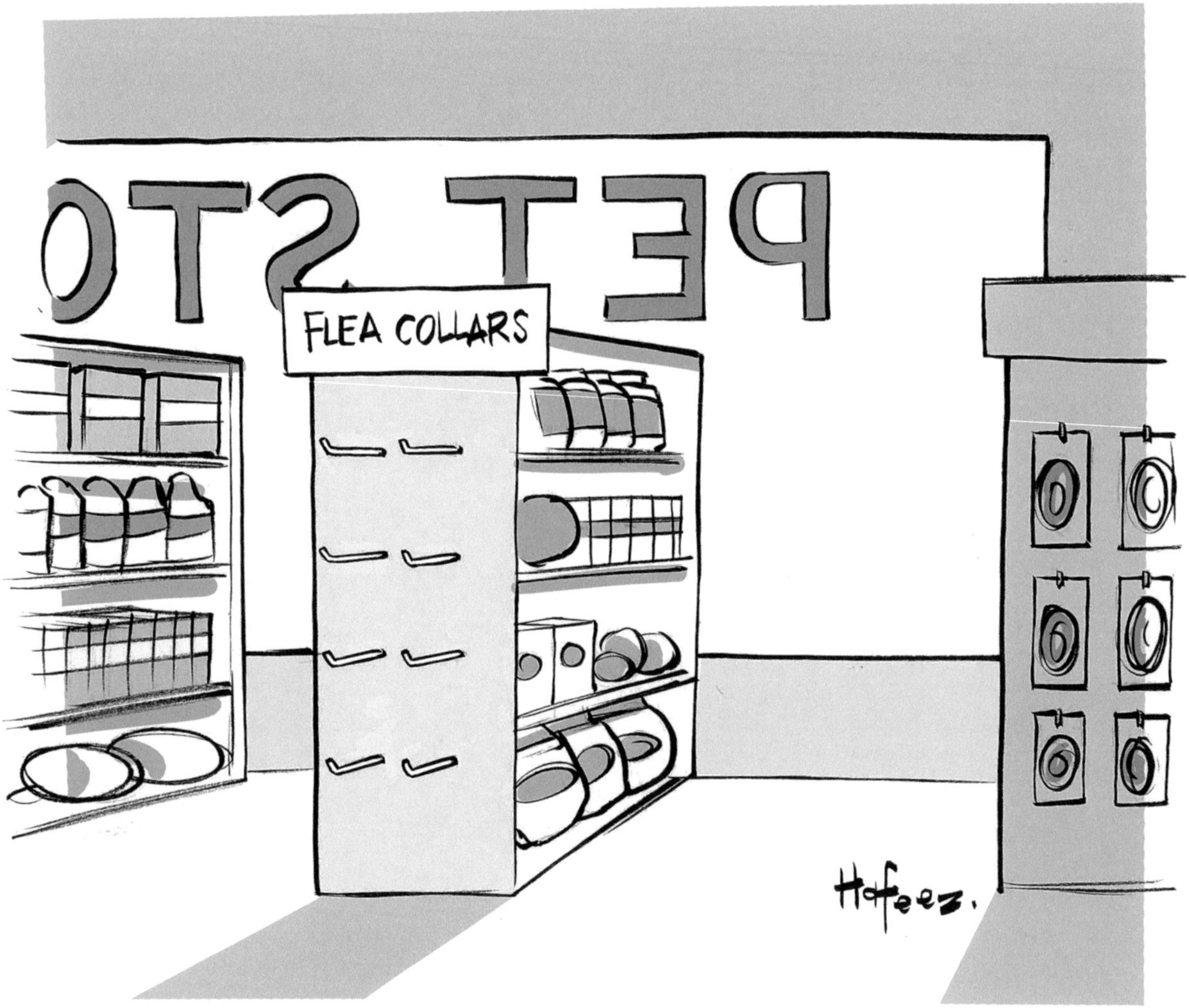
PET STO
FLEA COLLARS
Hafeez.

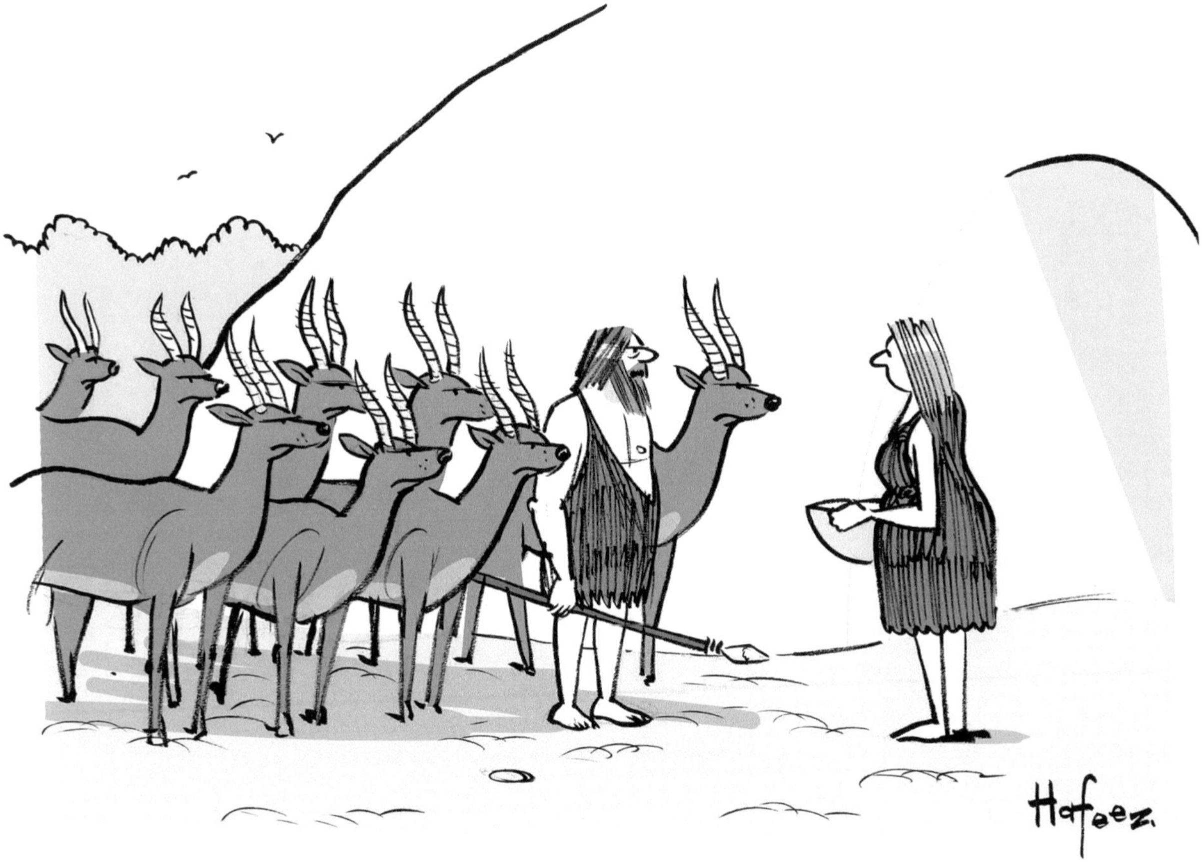
Hafeez

"I thought it was my turn to gather."

Moses
@Moses

TWEETS	FOLLOWING	FOLLOWERS
10	1	600,000

Hafeez.

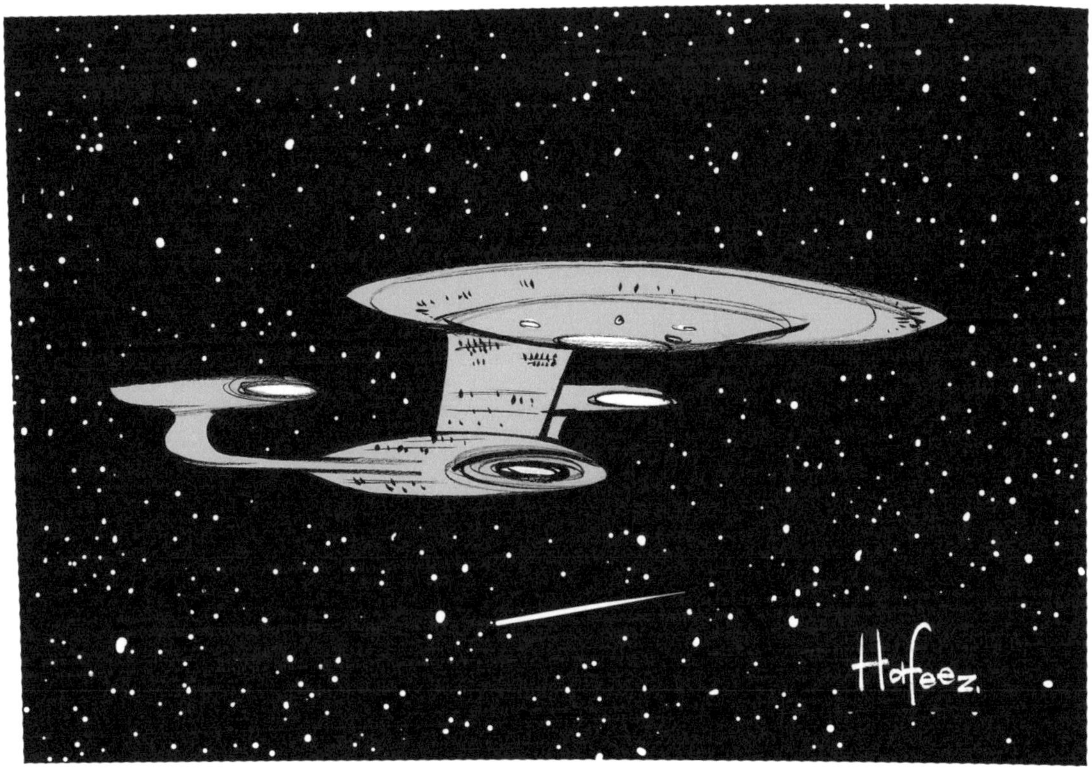
Hafeez.

THE iPhone 268s

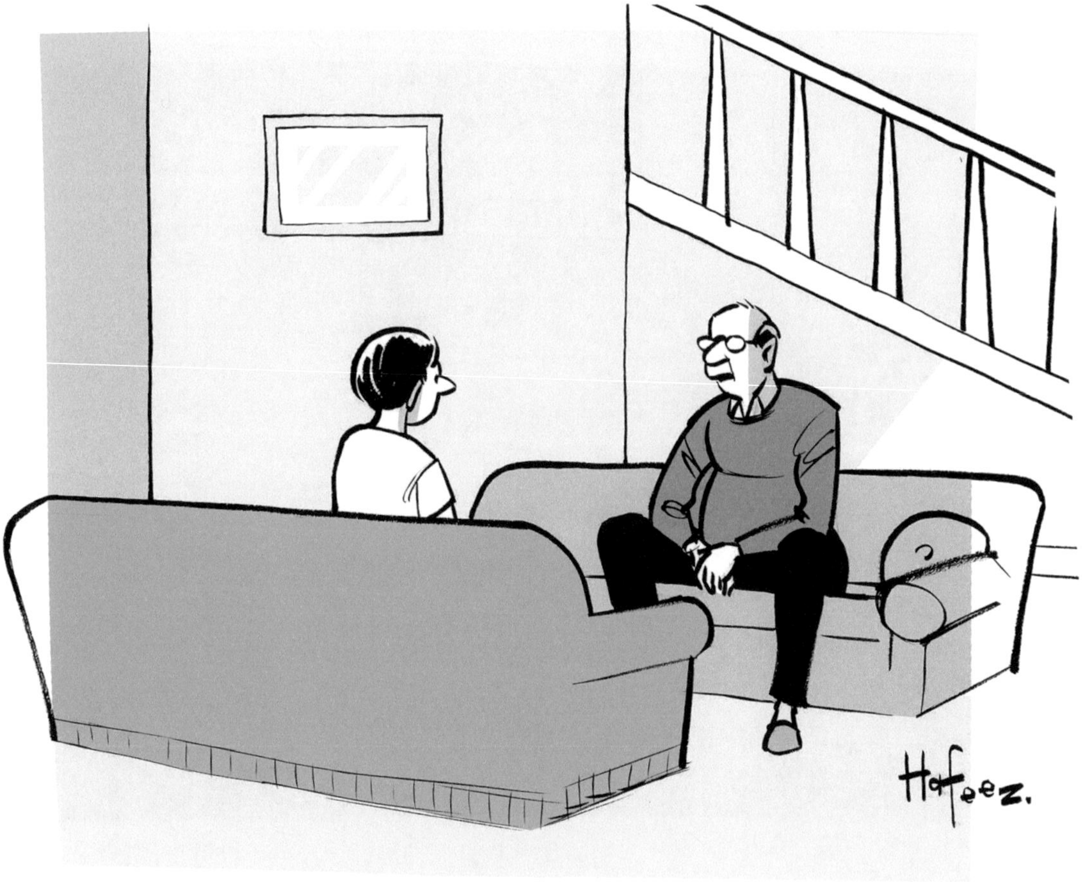
Hafeez.

"Your mother and I have an idea for your college savings plan—
how about taking some time off and enrolling in college
at the age of sixty-five?"

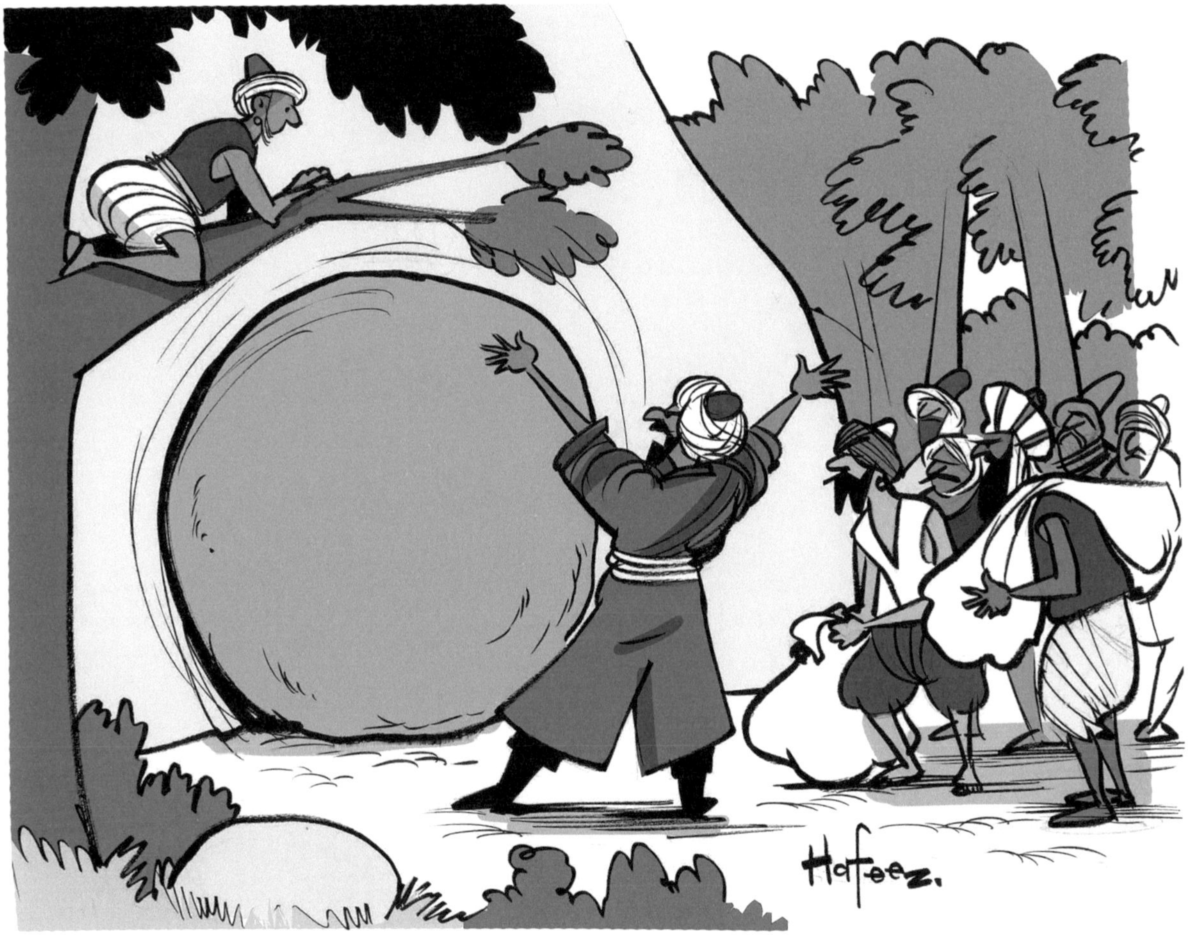
Hafeez.

"opEnsesaMe#7."

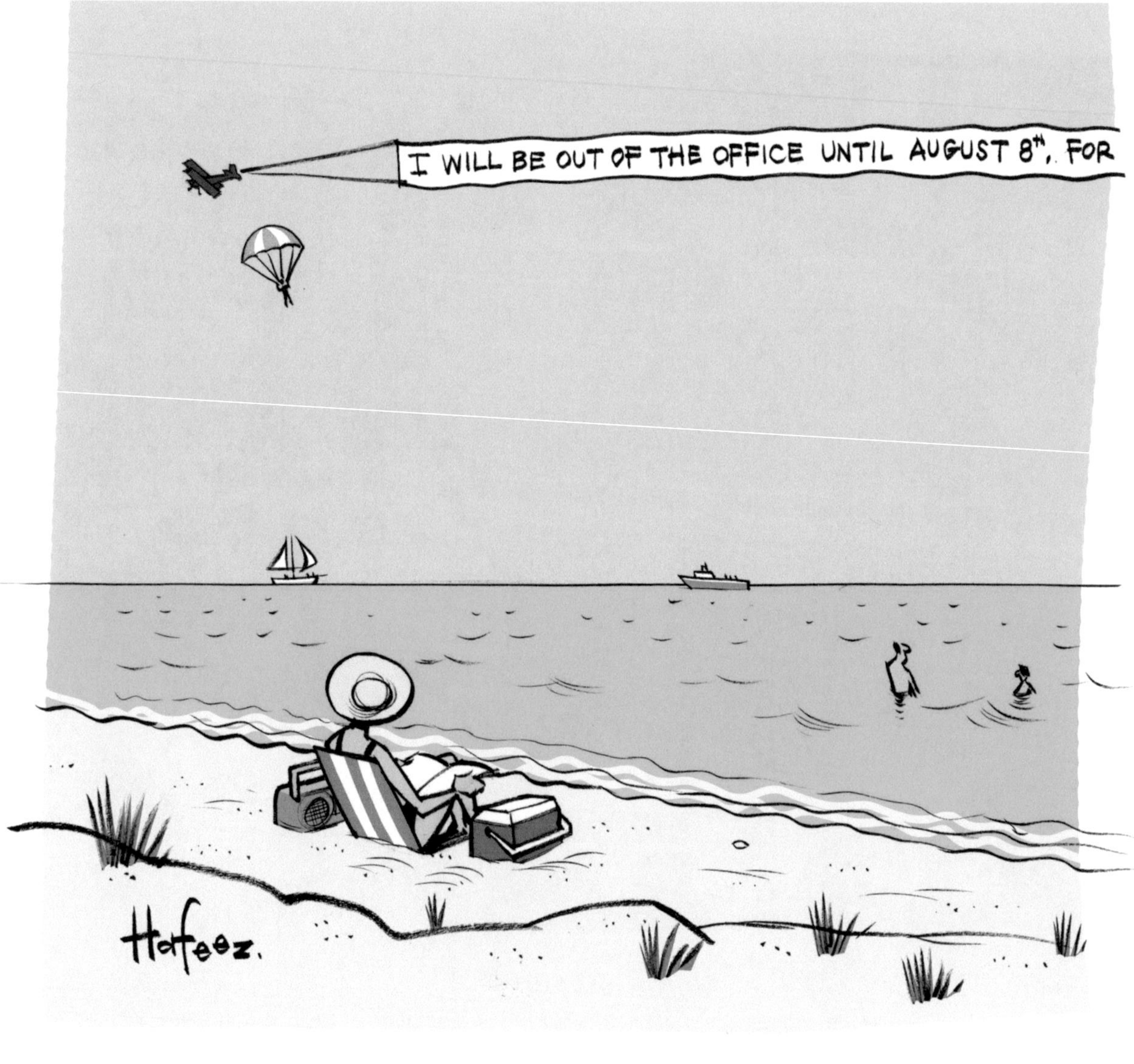
I WILL BE OUT OF THE OFFICE UNTIL AUGUST 8th, FOR
Hafeez.

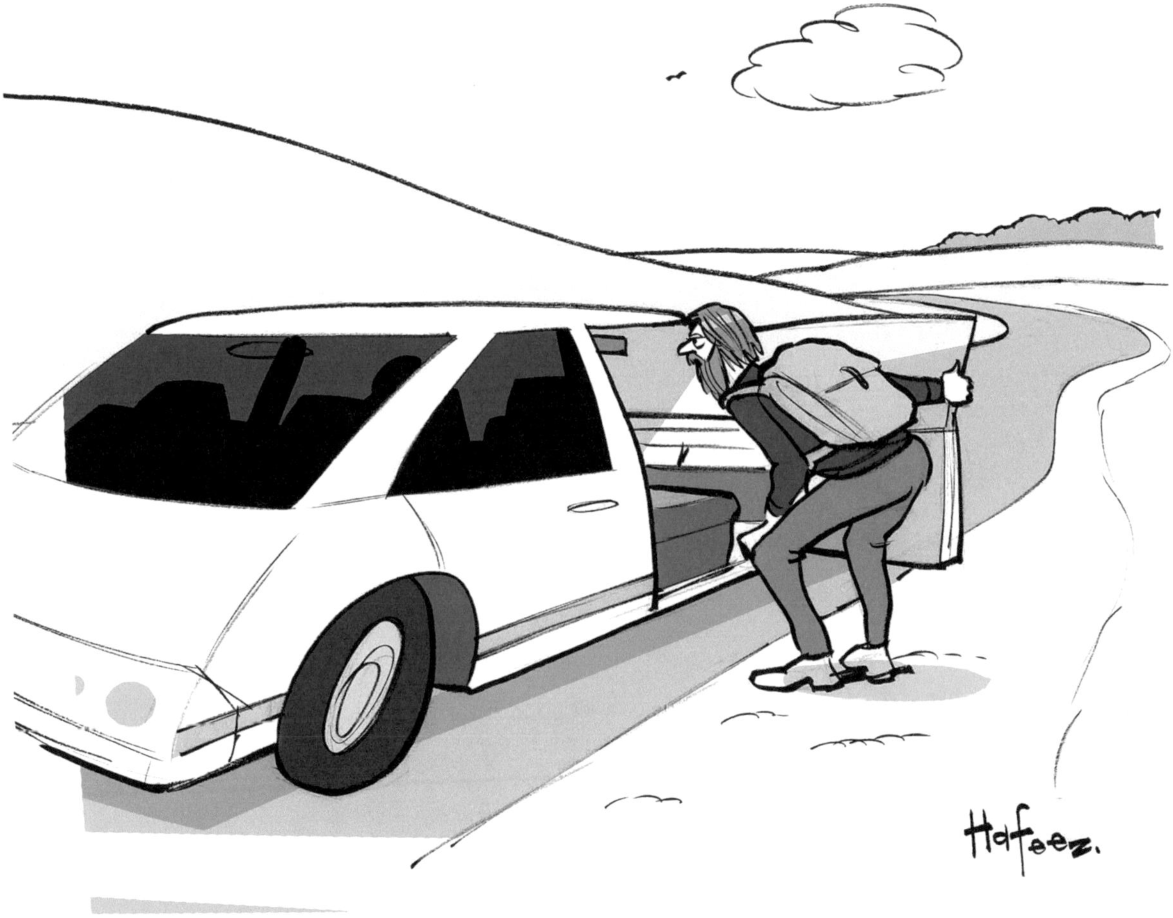
Hafeez.

"I don't need a lift—I was just 'Liking' your car."

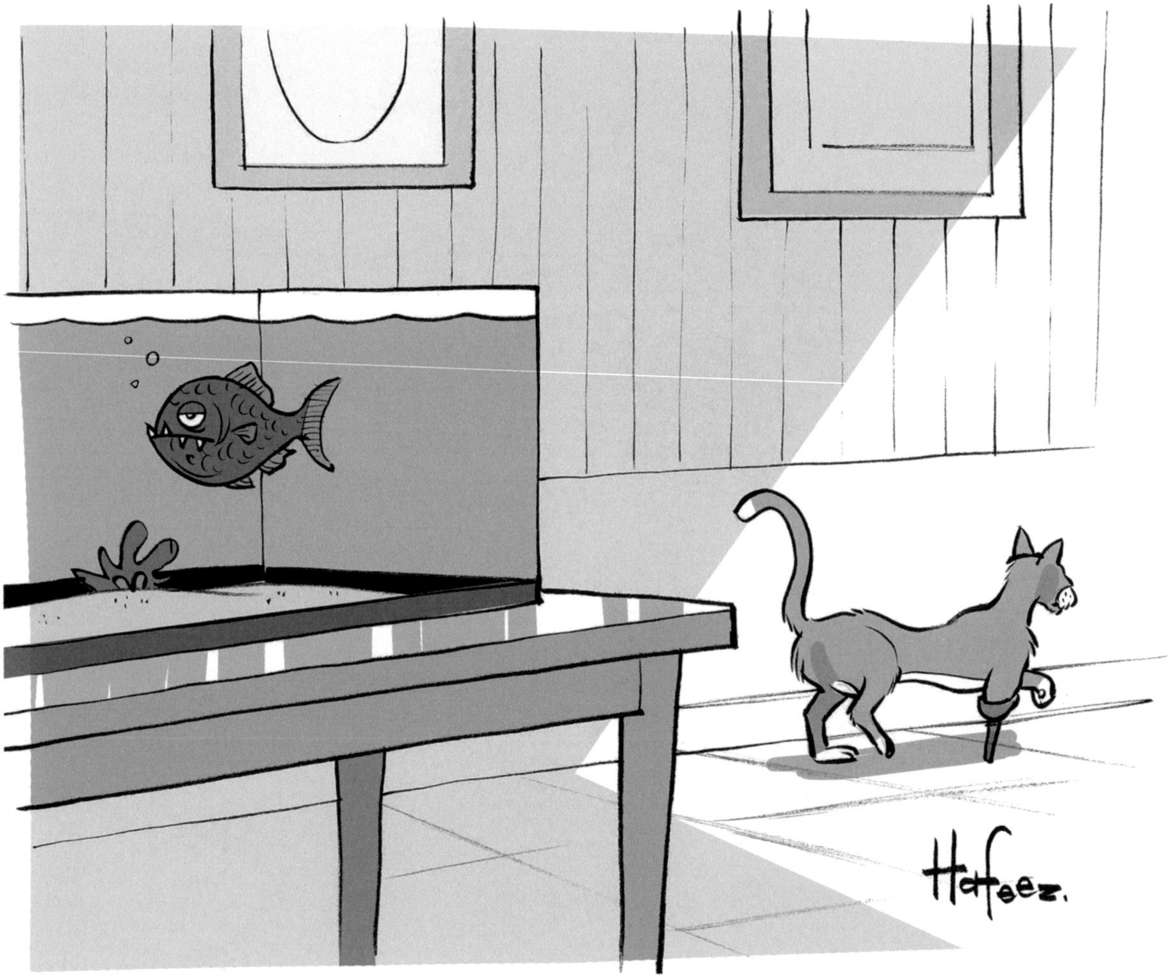
Hafeez.

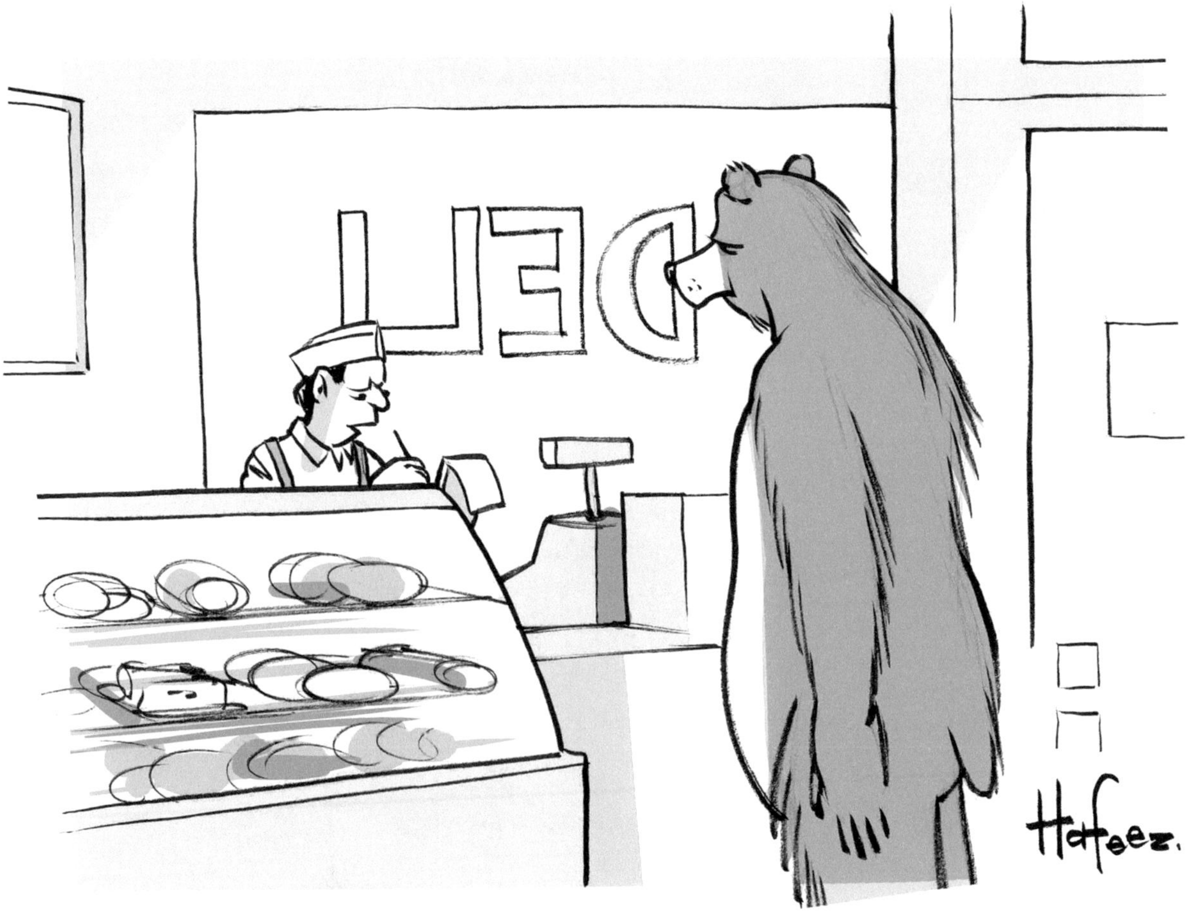
Hafeez.

"So that's one bagel with lox and cream cheese—hold the cream cheese, hold the bagel."

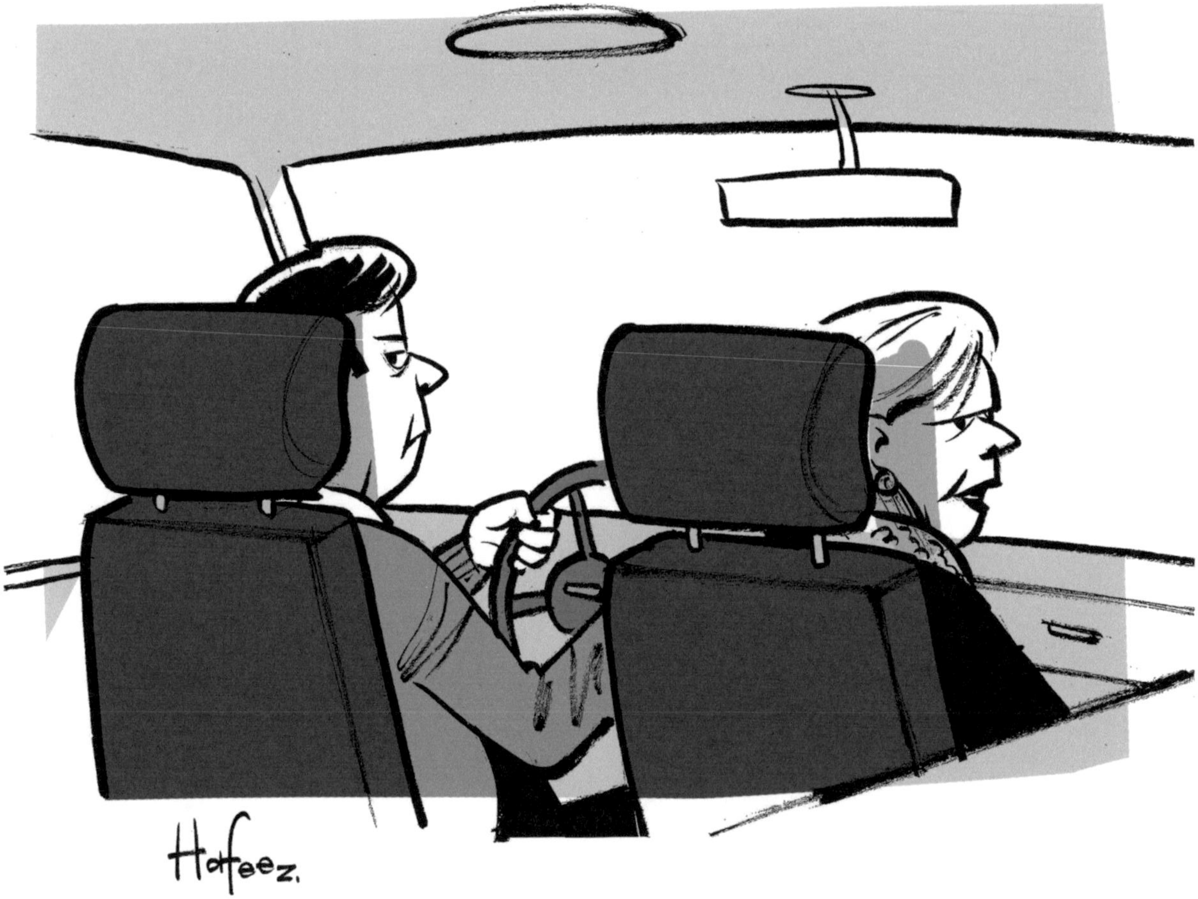
Hafeez.

"Oh look, honey, IKEA—where we had our first argument."

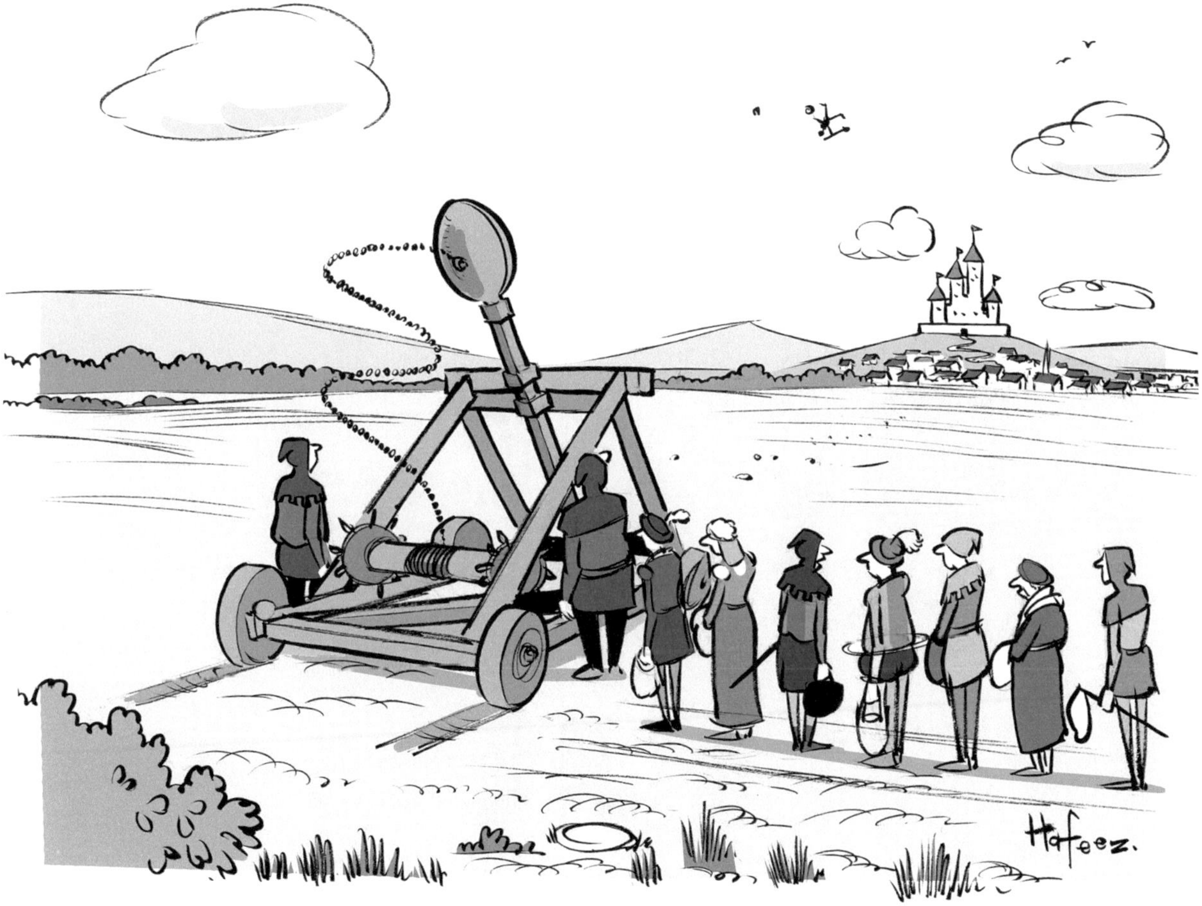
Hafeez.

"This commute is killing me."

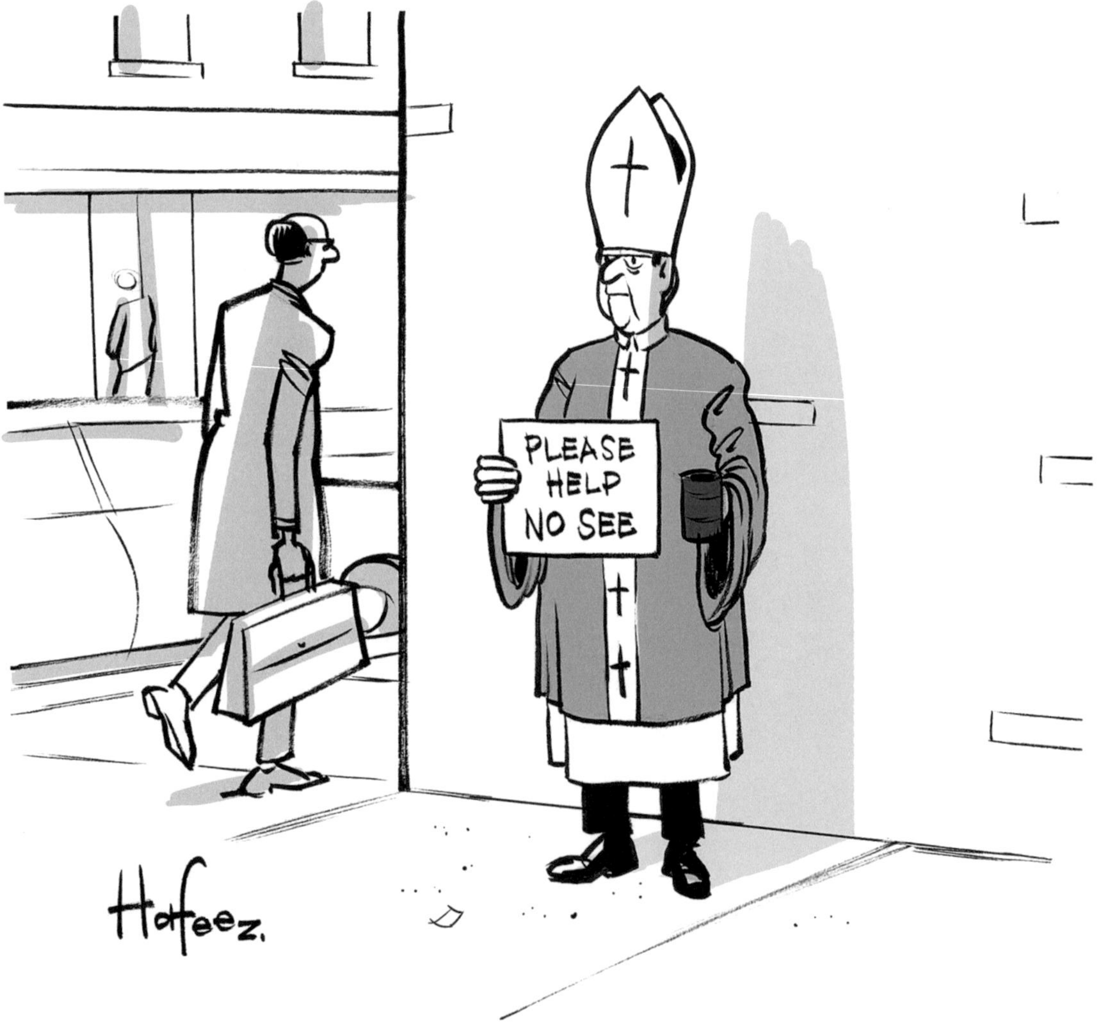
PLEASE
HELP
NO SEE
Hafeez.

"Do you have a few minutes to talk about the metric system?"

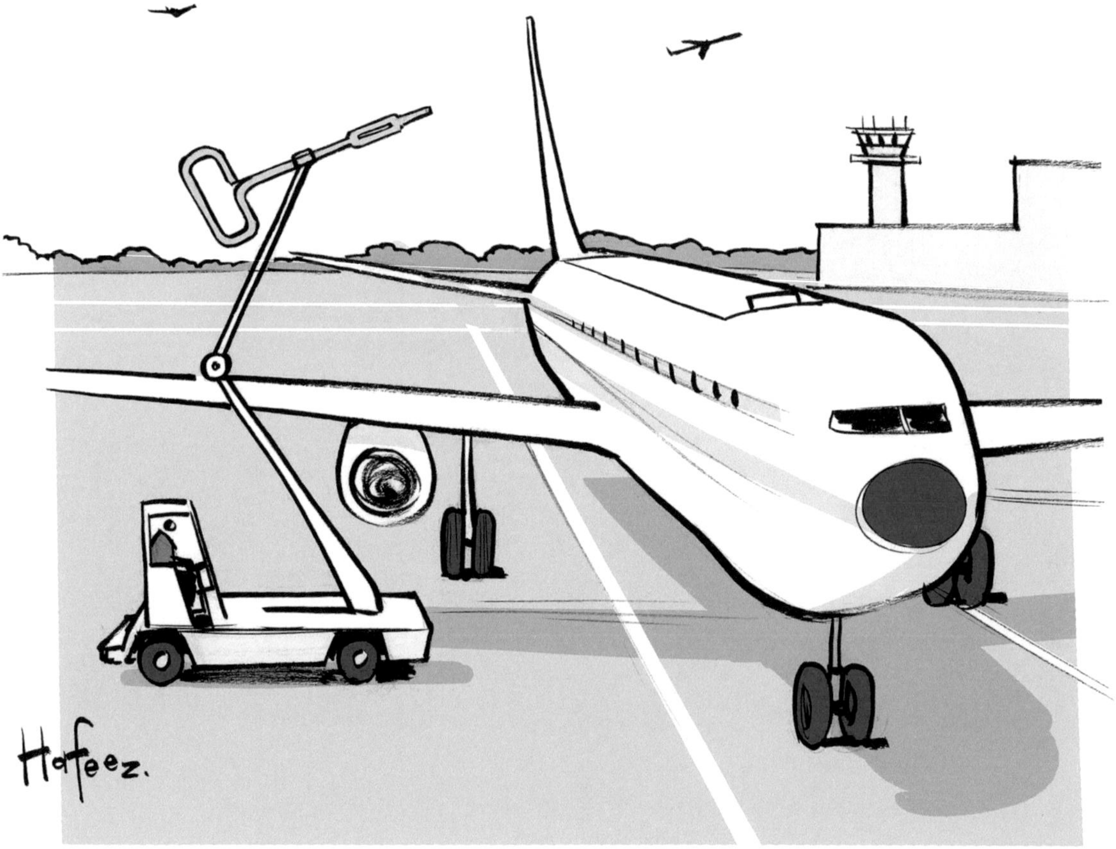
Hafeez.

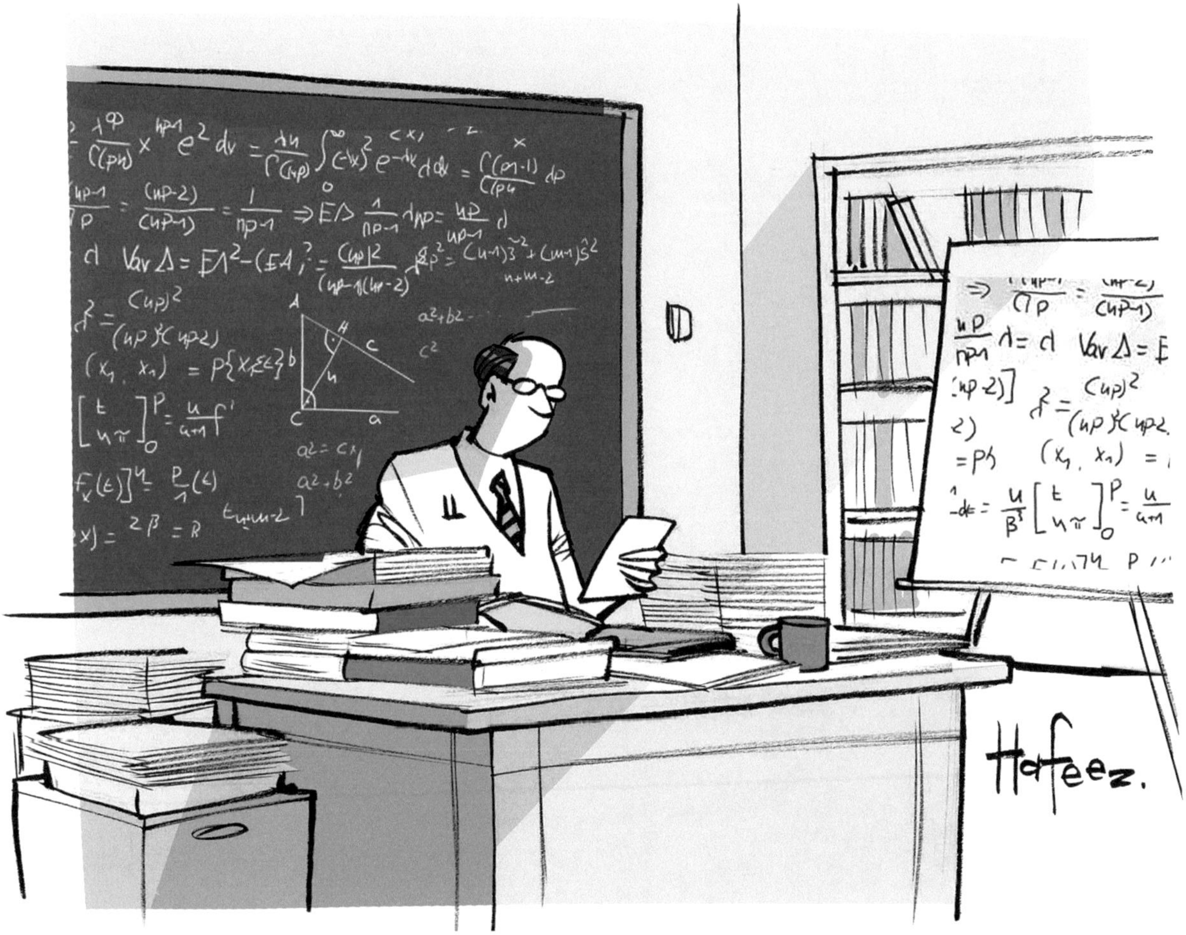
Hafeez.

"Thank you for submitting the enclosed research paper. Unfortunately, it did not pass our laugh test."

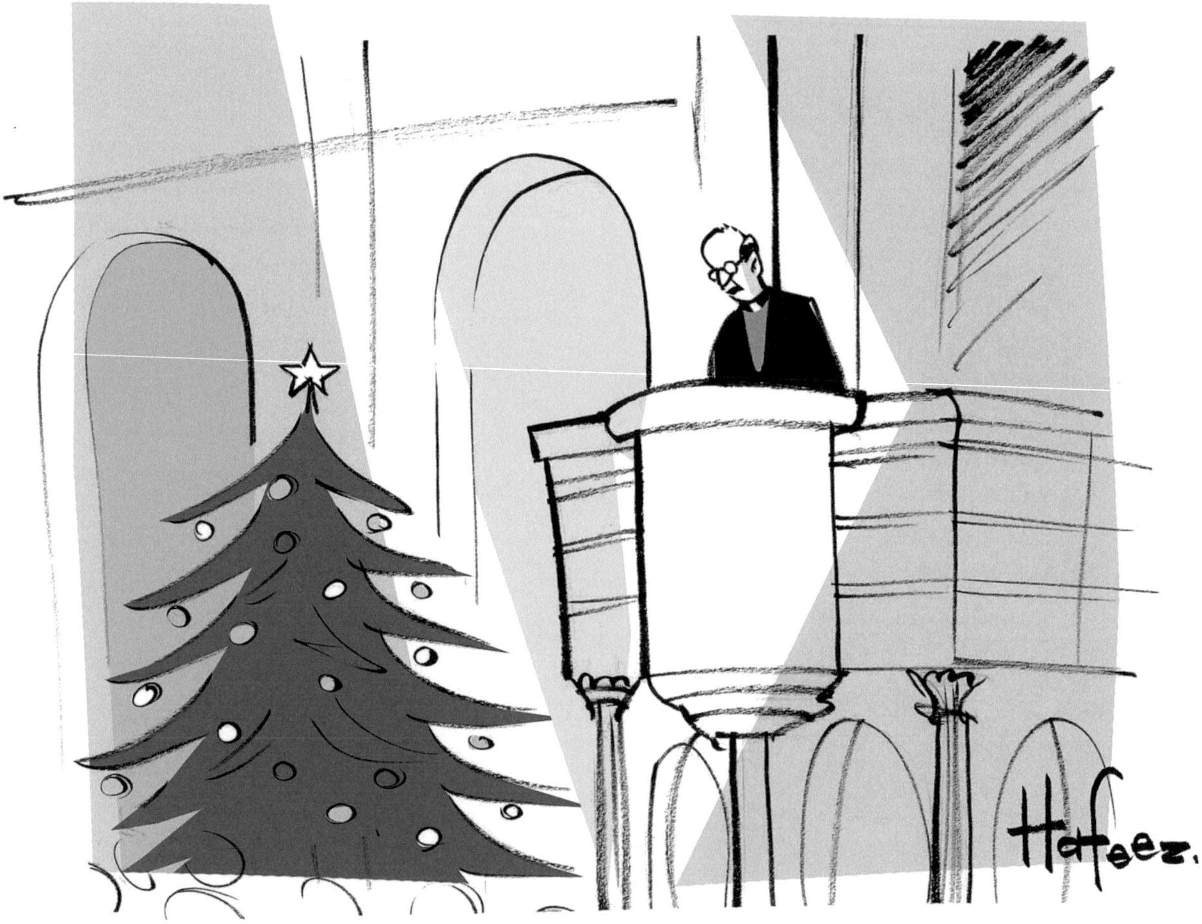
Hafeez.

"A Priest, a Wise Man, and a Magus walk into a barn ..."

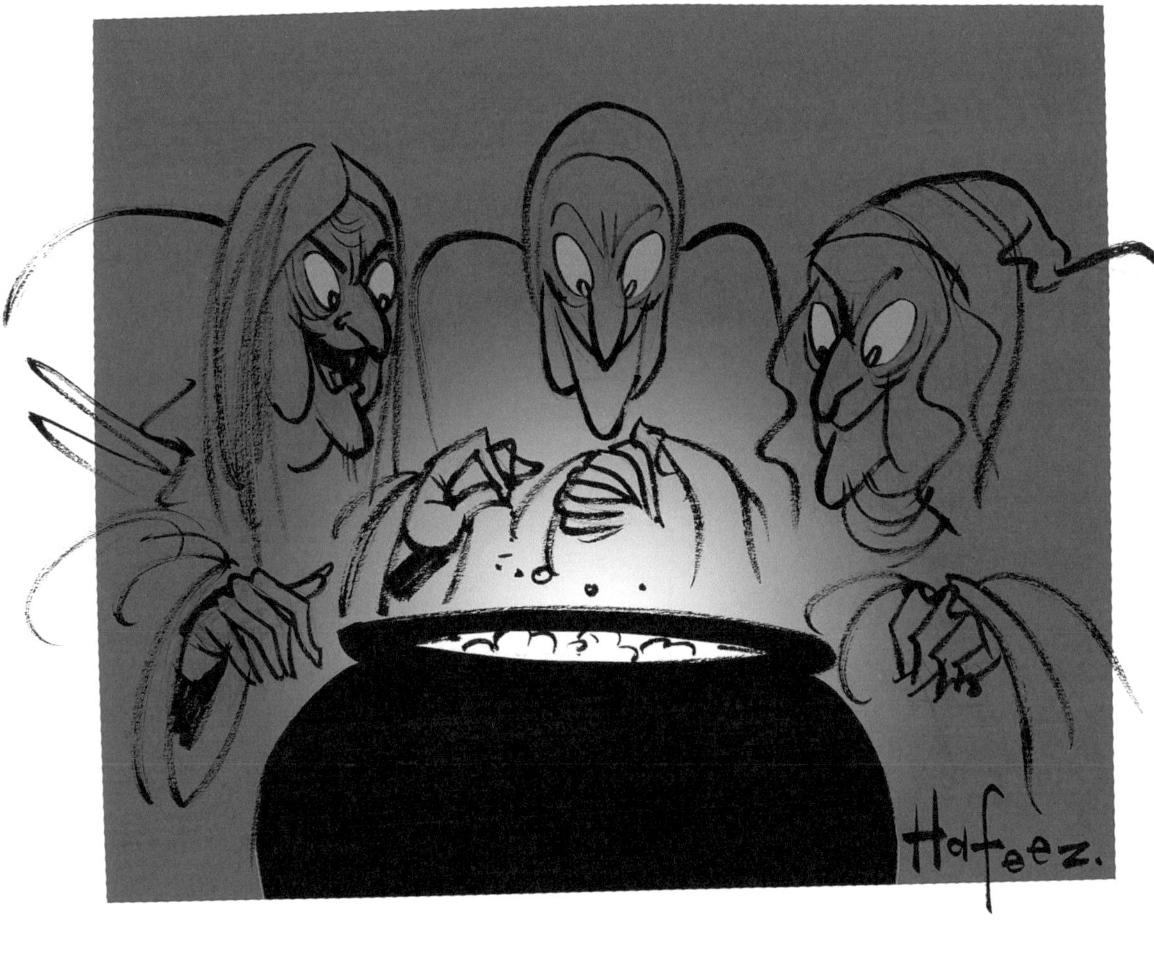
Hafeez.

"Double, double, toil and trouble,
Fire burn and Botox™ bubble."

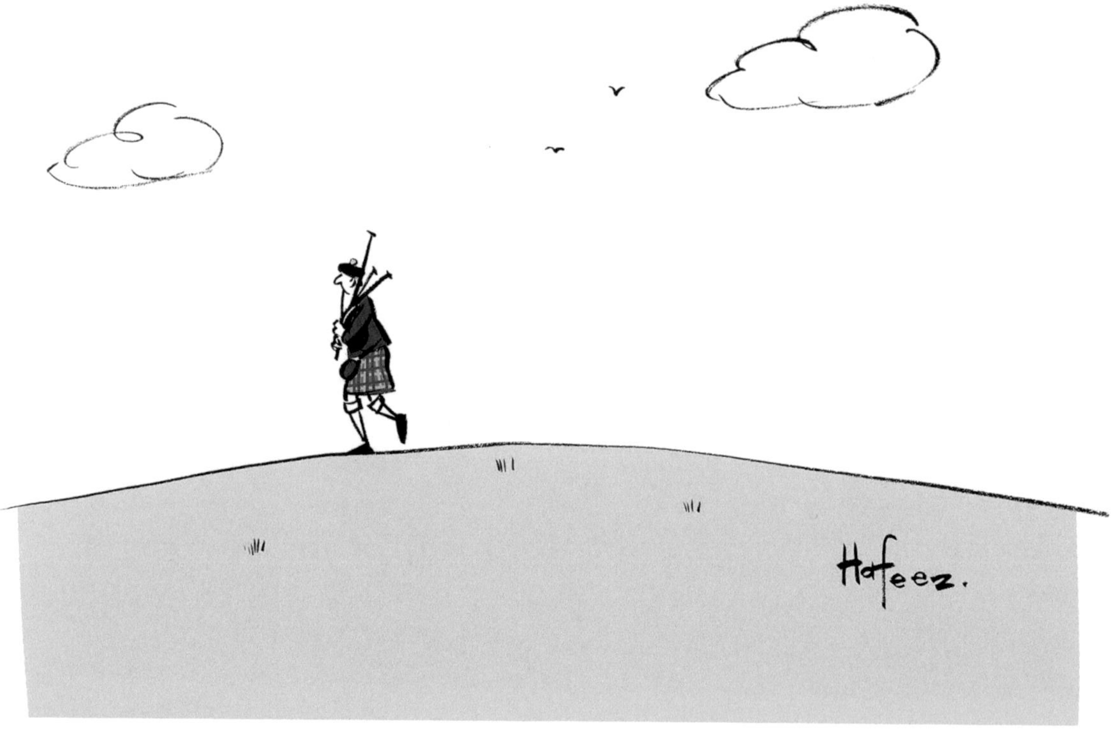
Hafeez.

THE PIED BAGPIPER

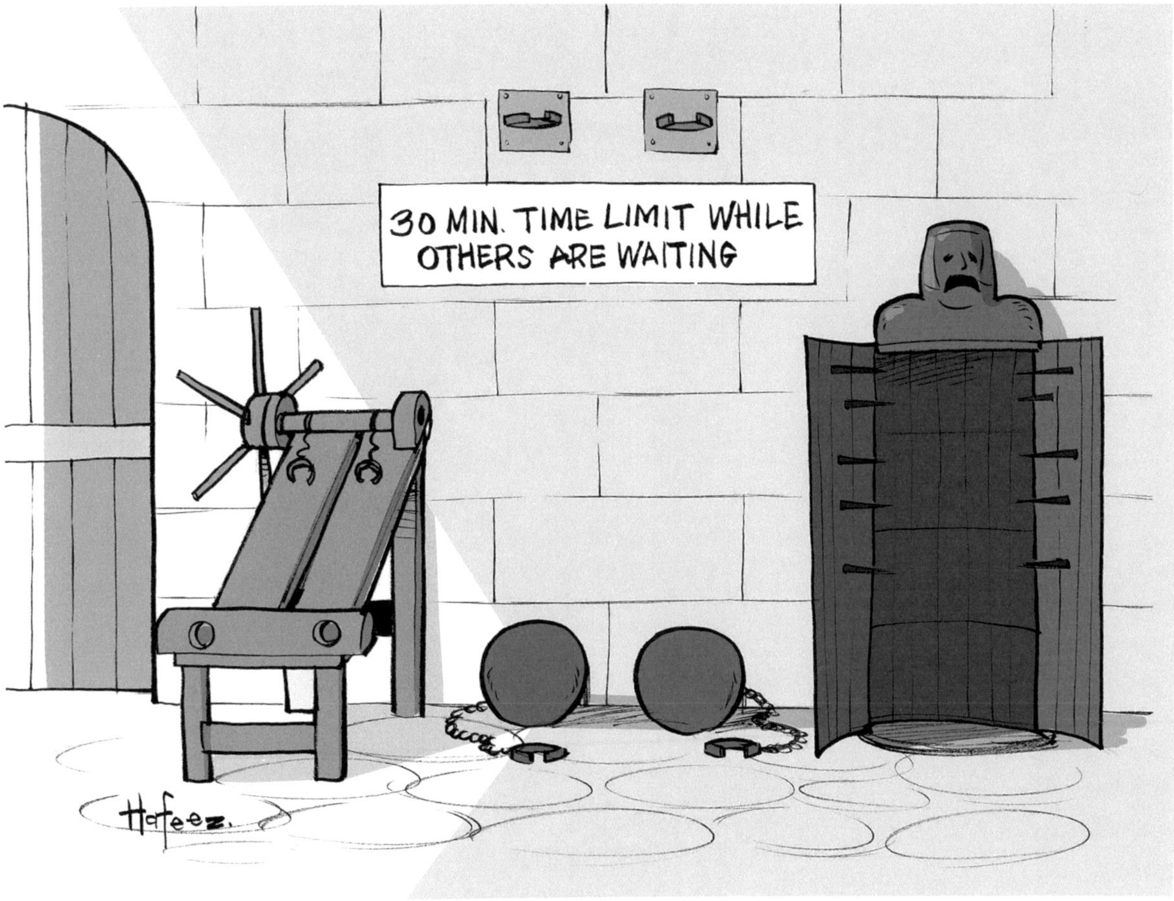
30 MIN. TIME LIMIT WHILE
OTHERS ARE WAITING
Hafeez.

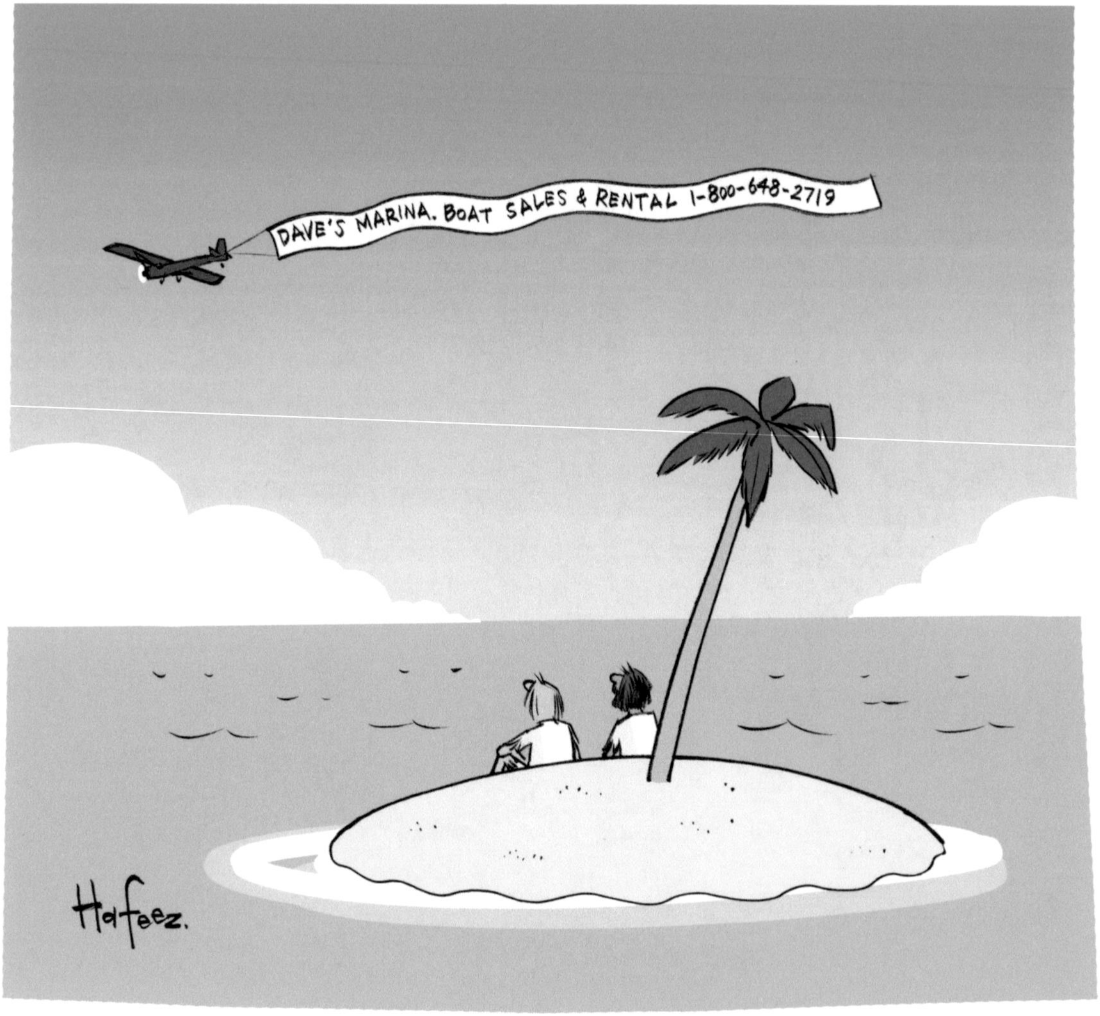
DAVE'S MARINA. BOAT SALES & RENTAL 1-800-648-2719
Hafeez.

"There's no privacy anymore."

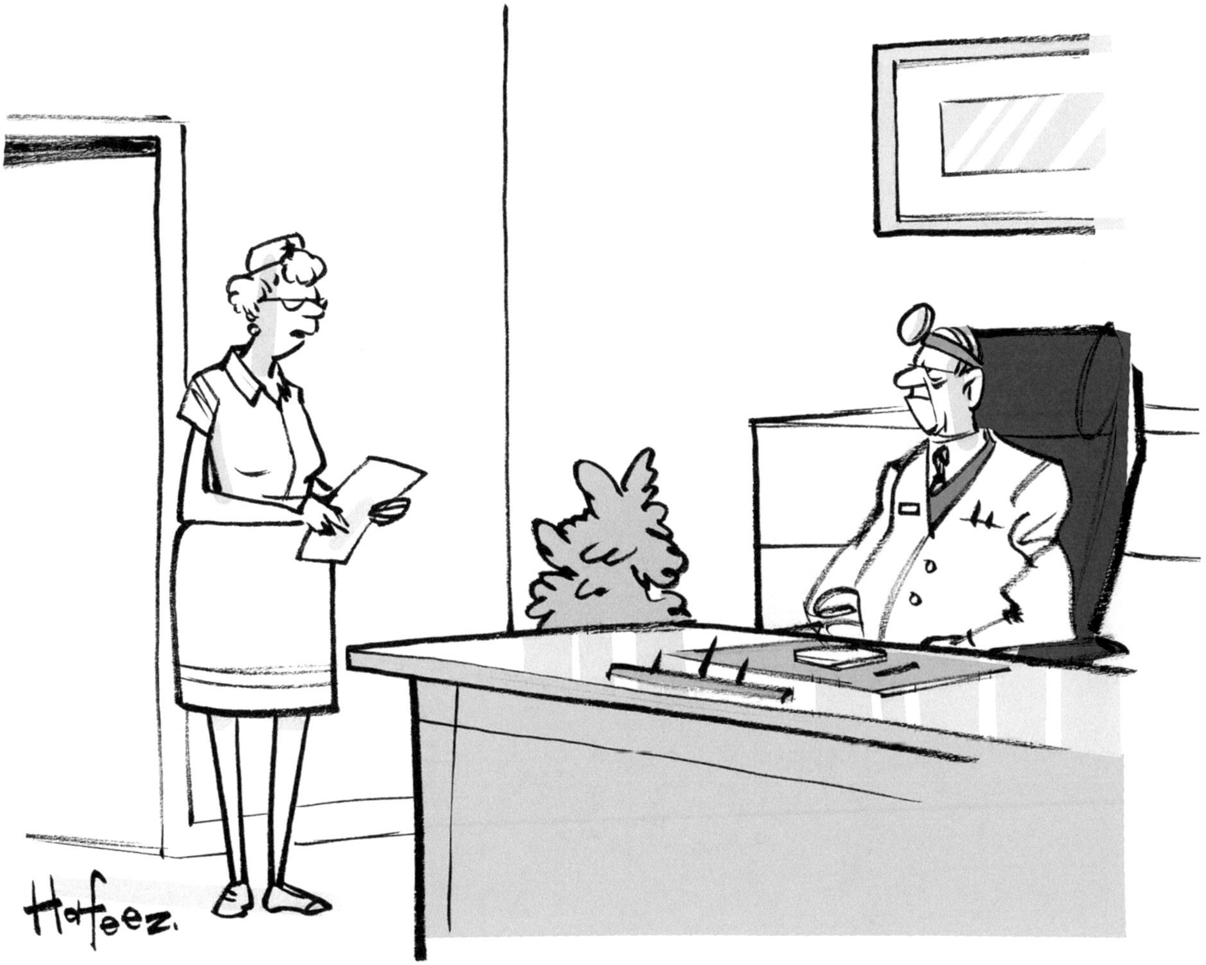
Hafeez.

"It's a warning from the American Hypochondriacs Association. Apparently you've been over-prescribing placebos."

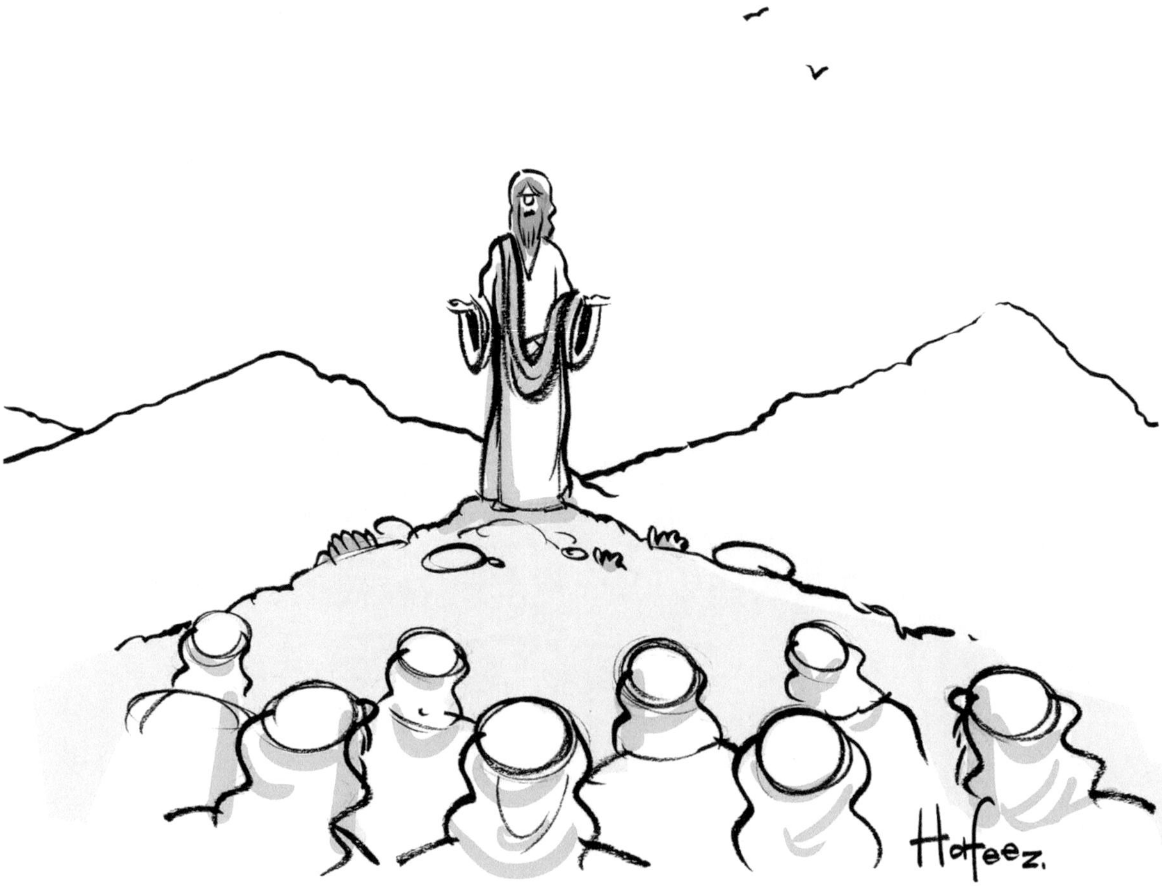
Hafeez.

"Blessed are the Greek, for they shall invent olive oil."

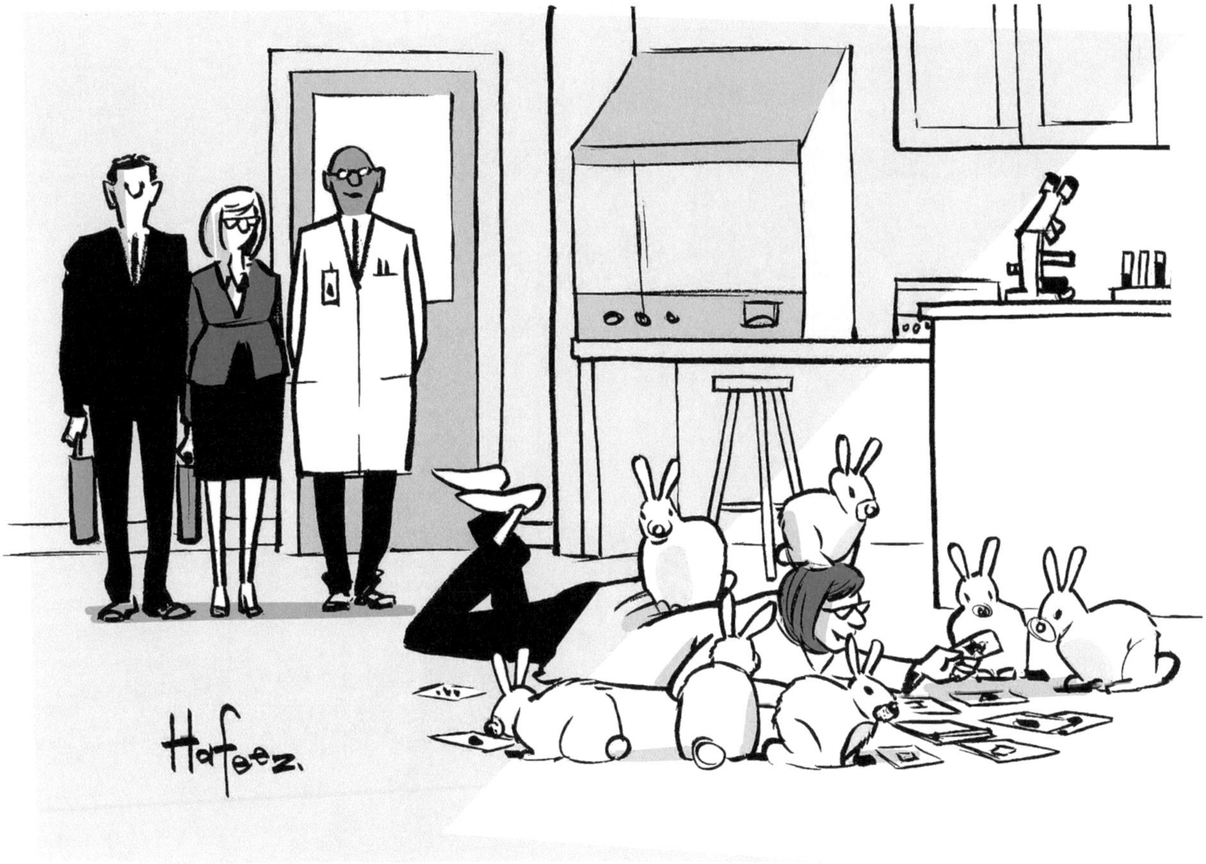
Hafeez.

"There's no animal testing in our lab. The emphasis is on group work and development of social skills."

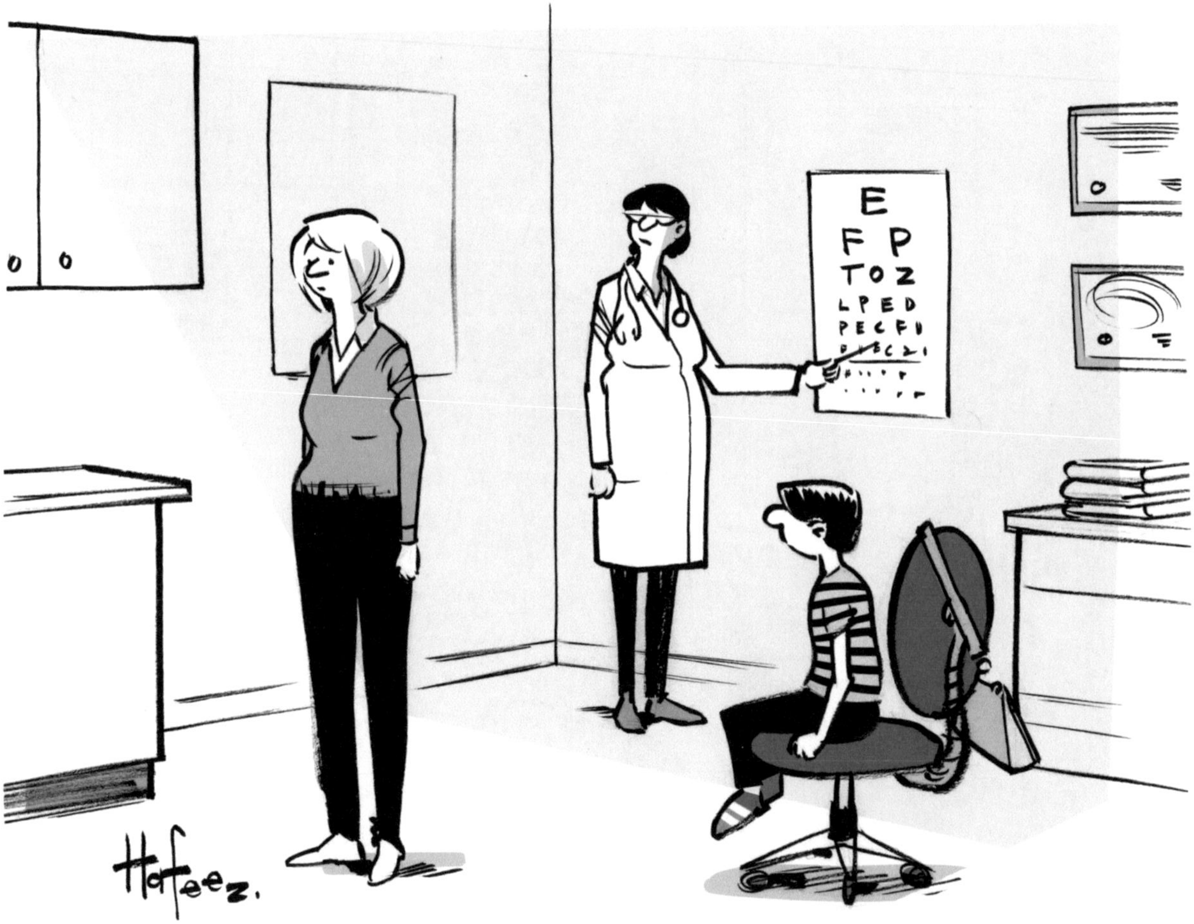
E
F P
T O Z
L P E D
Hafeez.

"How about this line?"

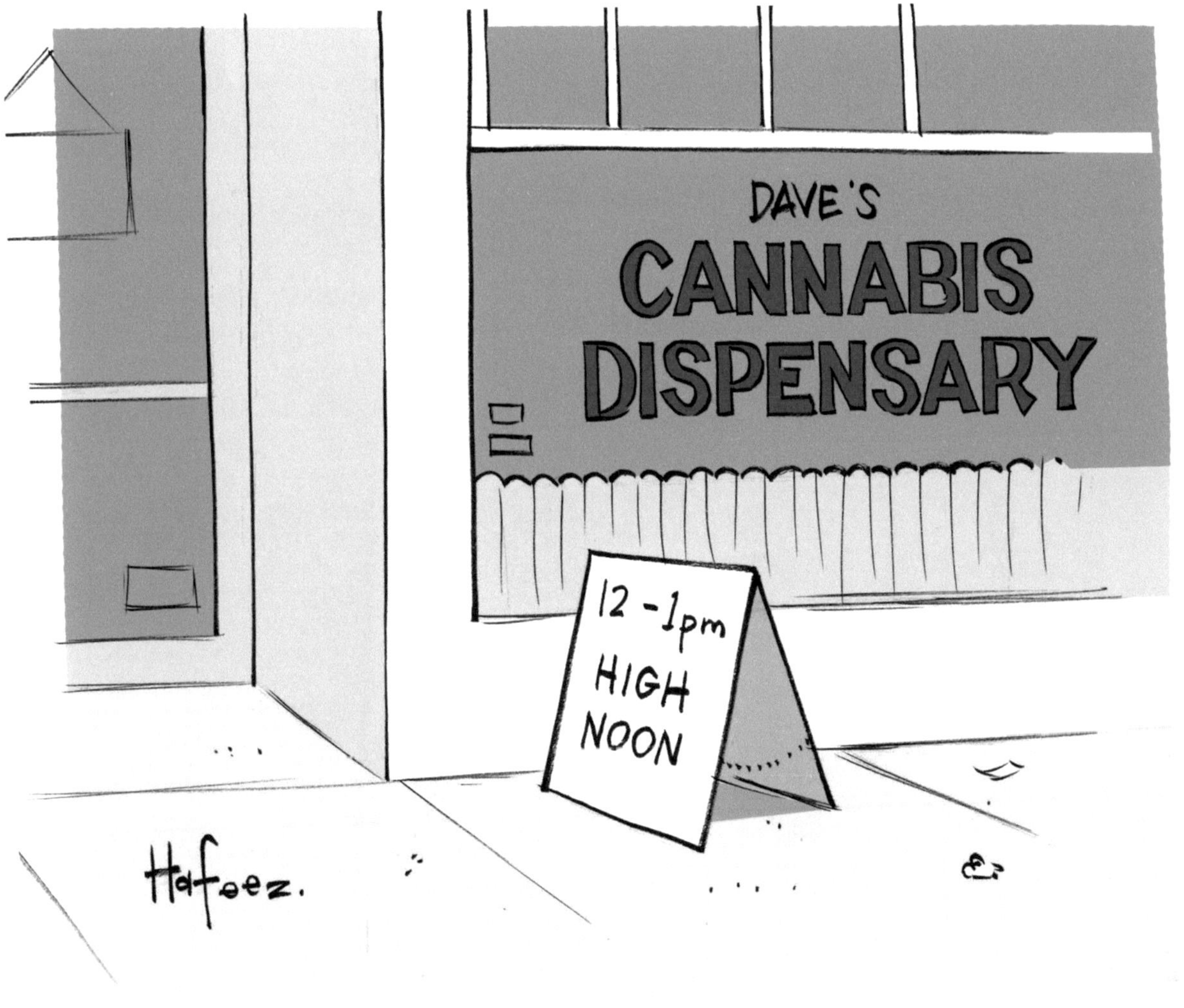
DAVE'S
CANNABIS
DISPENSARY
12 - 1pm
HIGH
NOON
Hafeez.

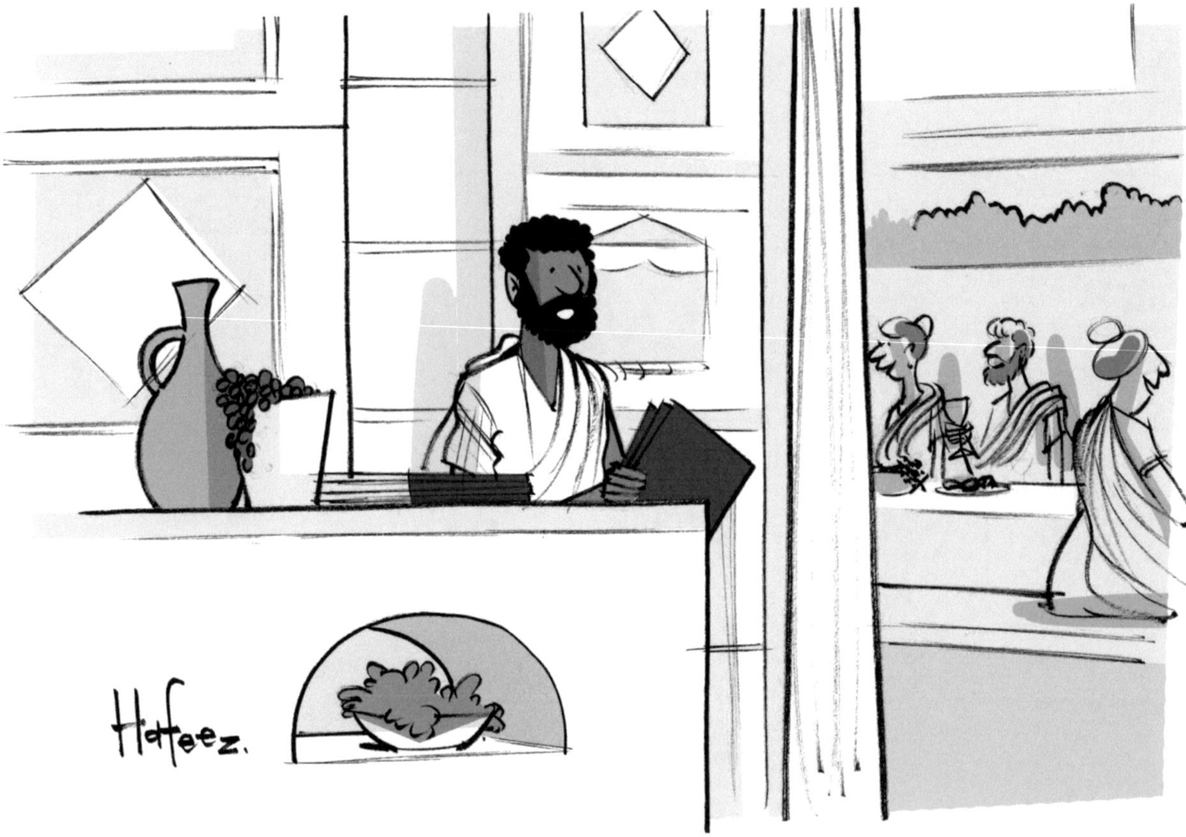
Hafeez.

"Christ, party of thirteen!"

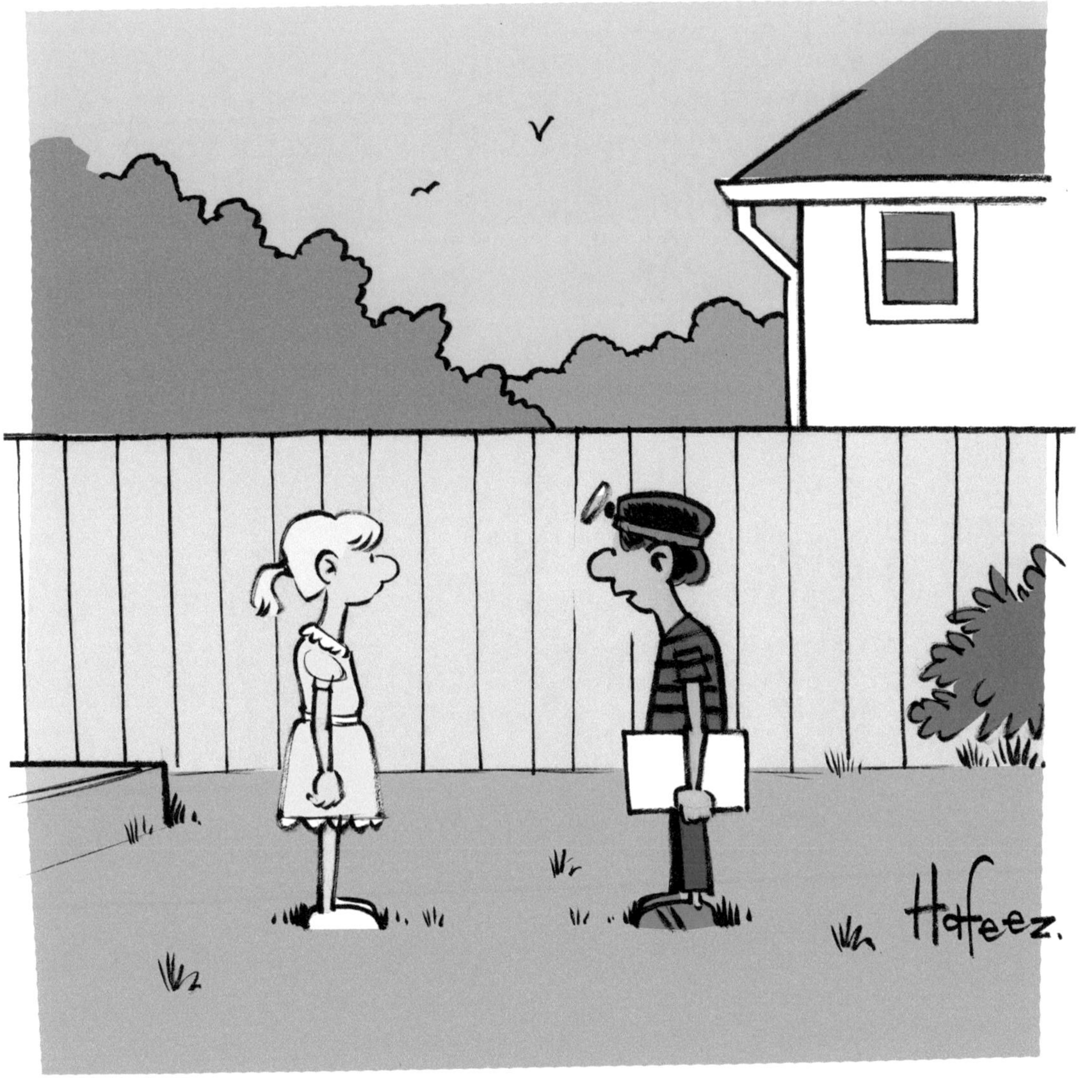
Hafeez.

"Let's play make-believe. I'll diagnose you with a life-threatening illness, then cure you with a wonder-drug that turns out to be a placebo."

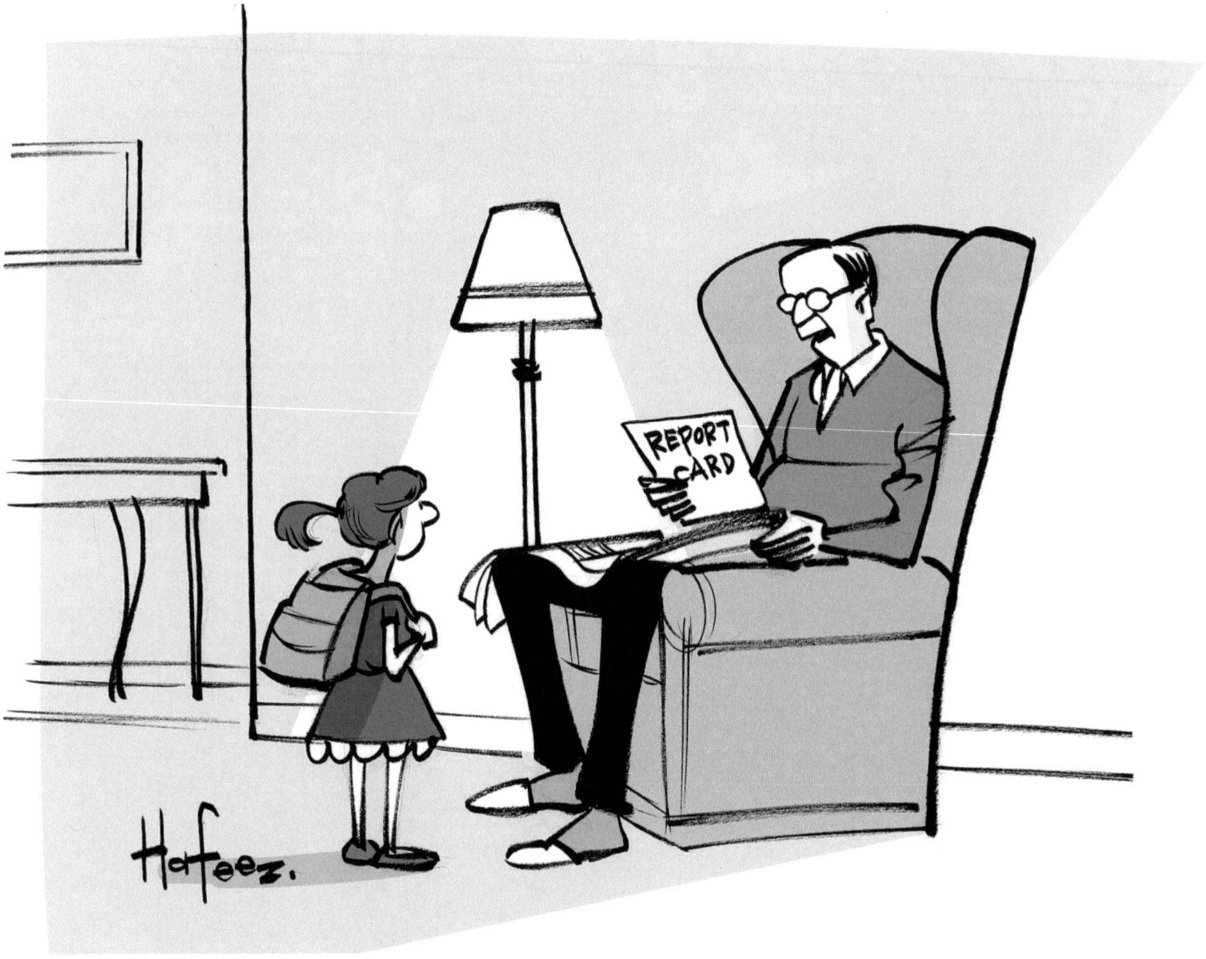
REPORT CARD
Hafeez.

"At least you're not afraid to fail."

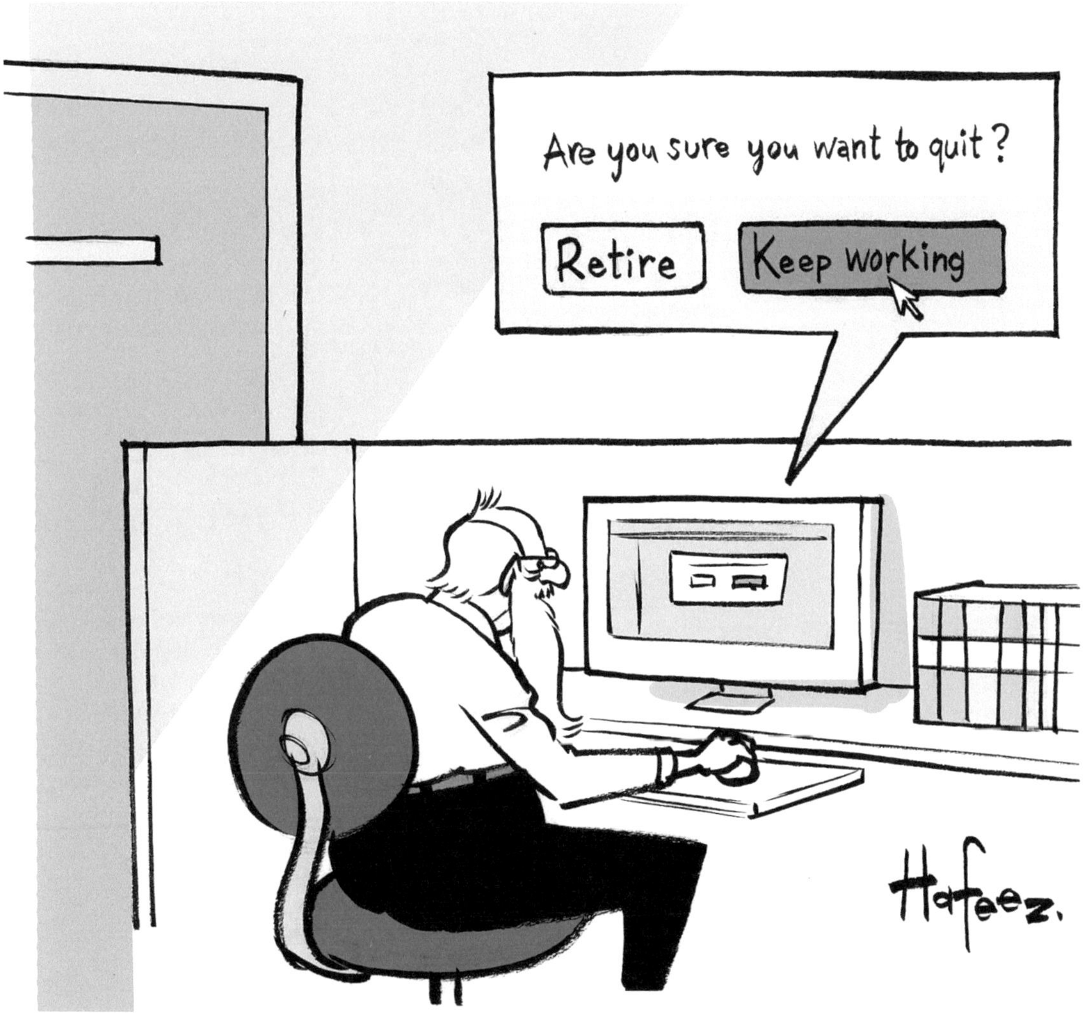
Are you sure you want to quit?
Retire
Keep working
Hafeez.

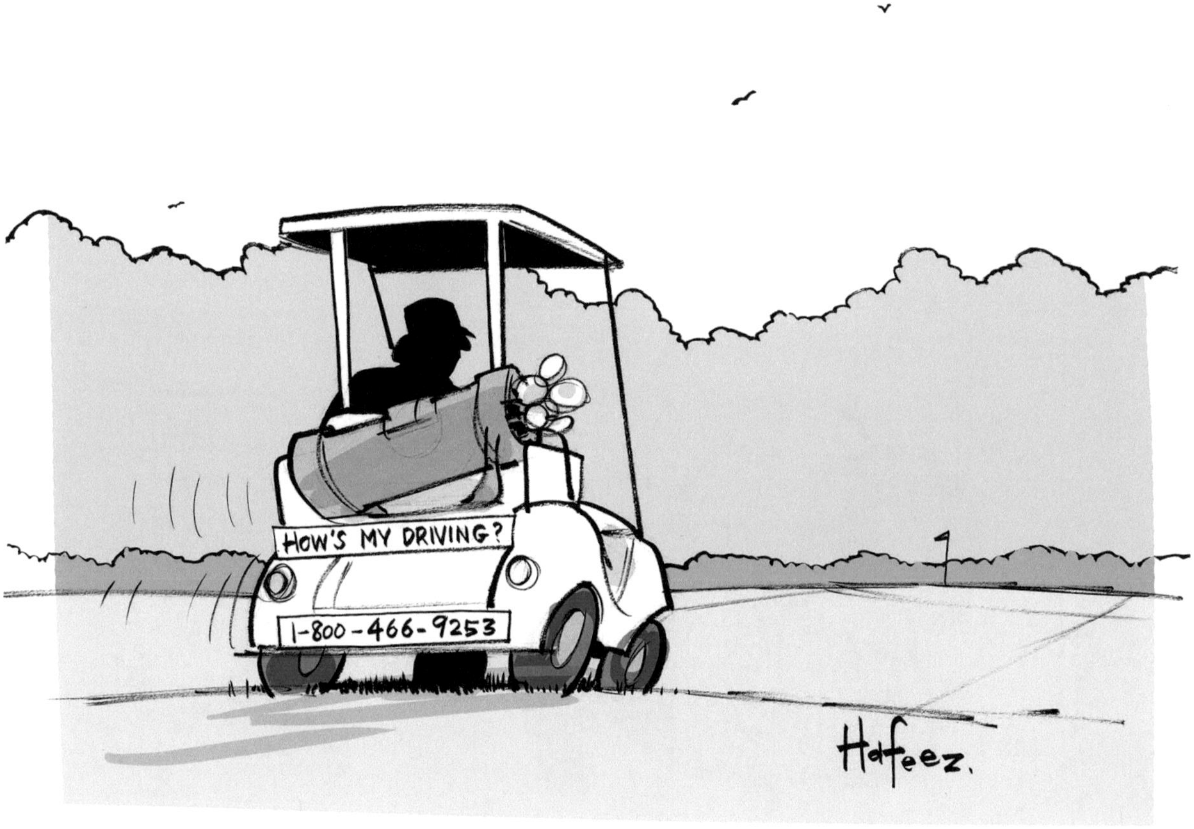
HOW'S MY DRIVING?
1-800-466-9253
Hafeez.

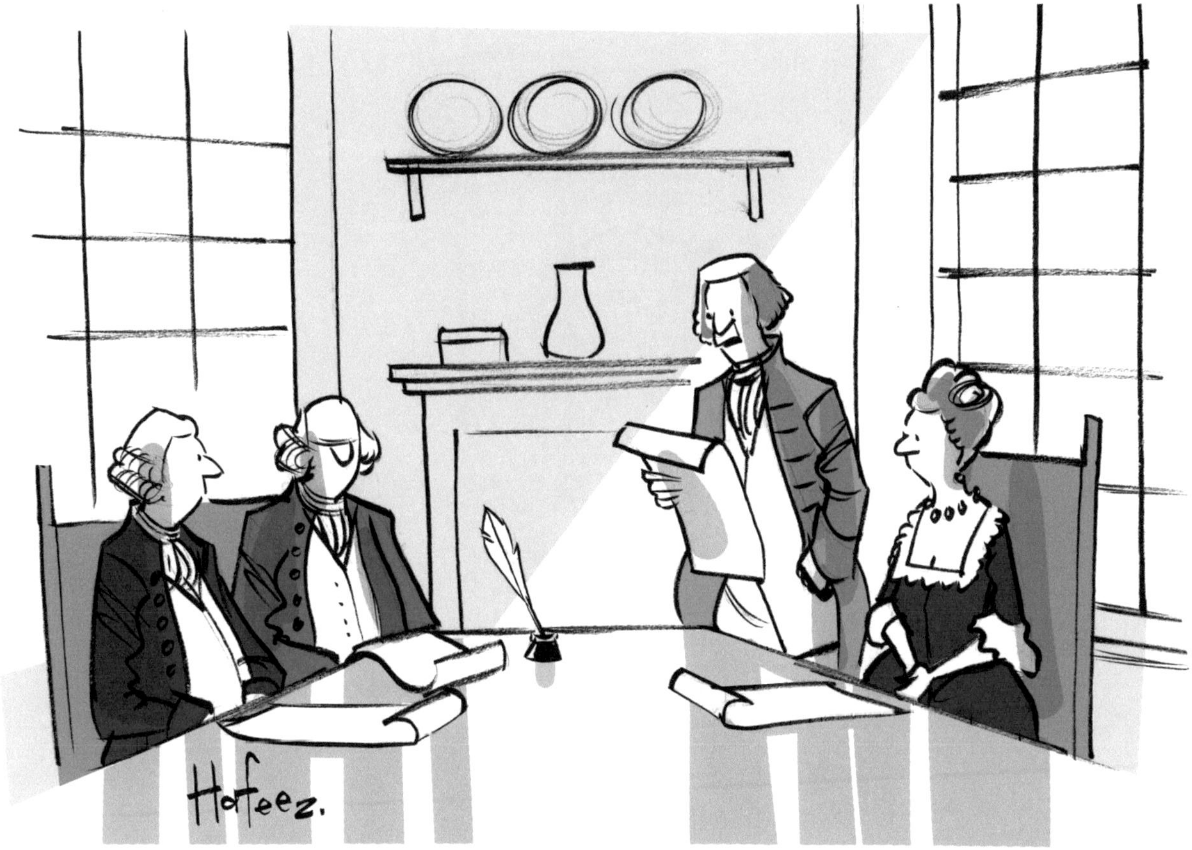
Hafeez.

"When in the Course of human events, it becomes necessary for one person to dissolve the marital bonds which have connected her with another, ..."

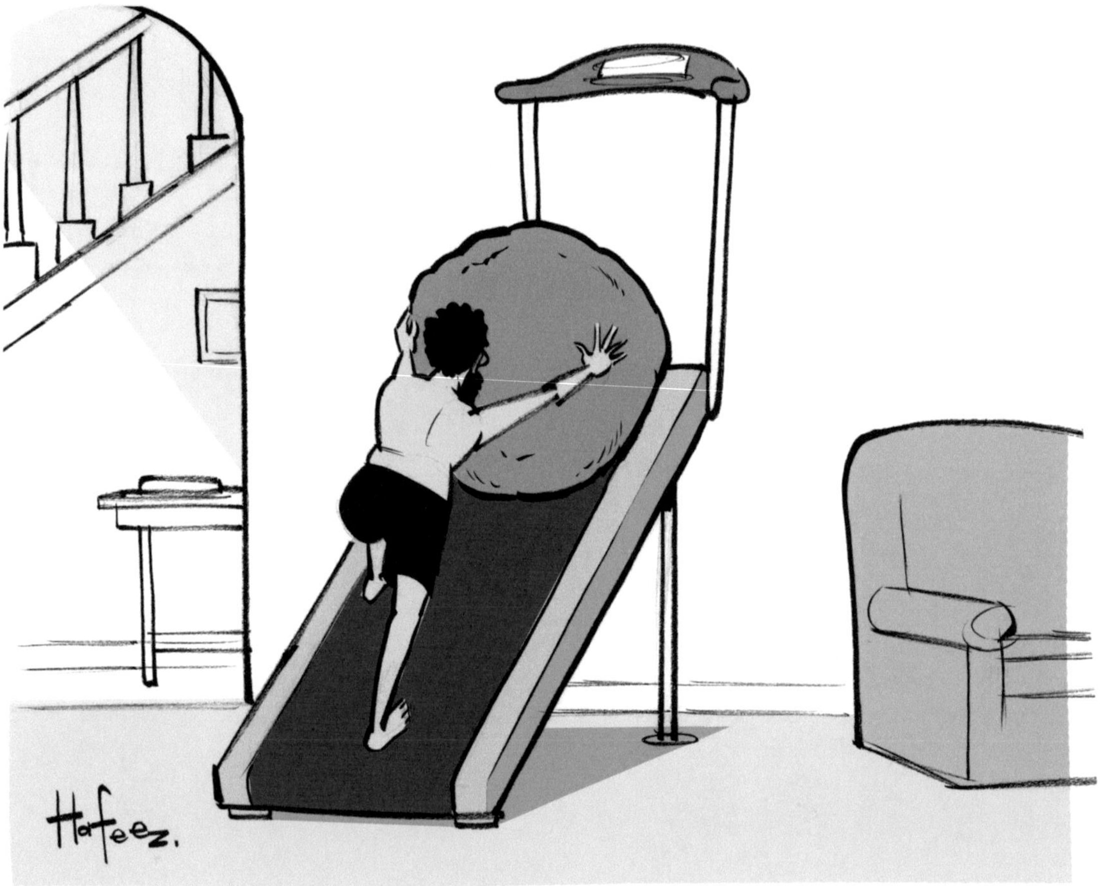
Hafeez.

THE ETERNITY WORKOUT

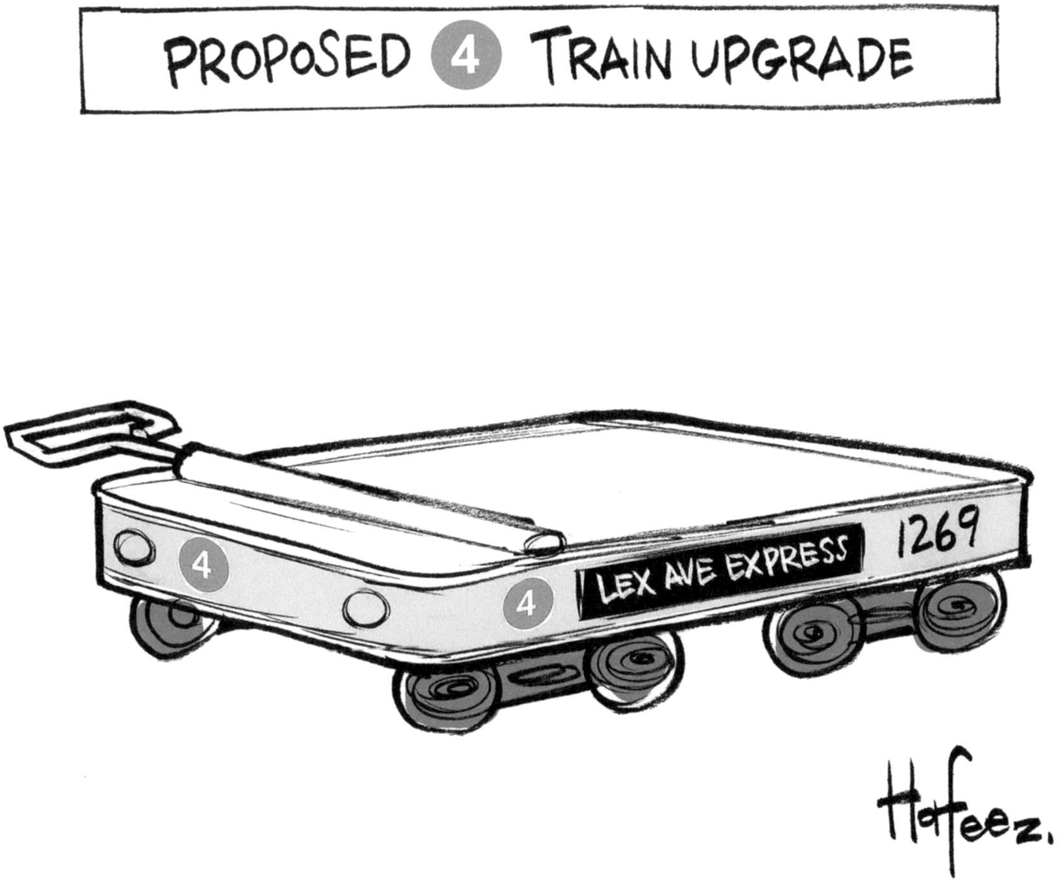
PROPOSED 4 TRAIN UPGRADE
4
4
LEX AVE EXPRESS
1269
Hafeez.

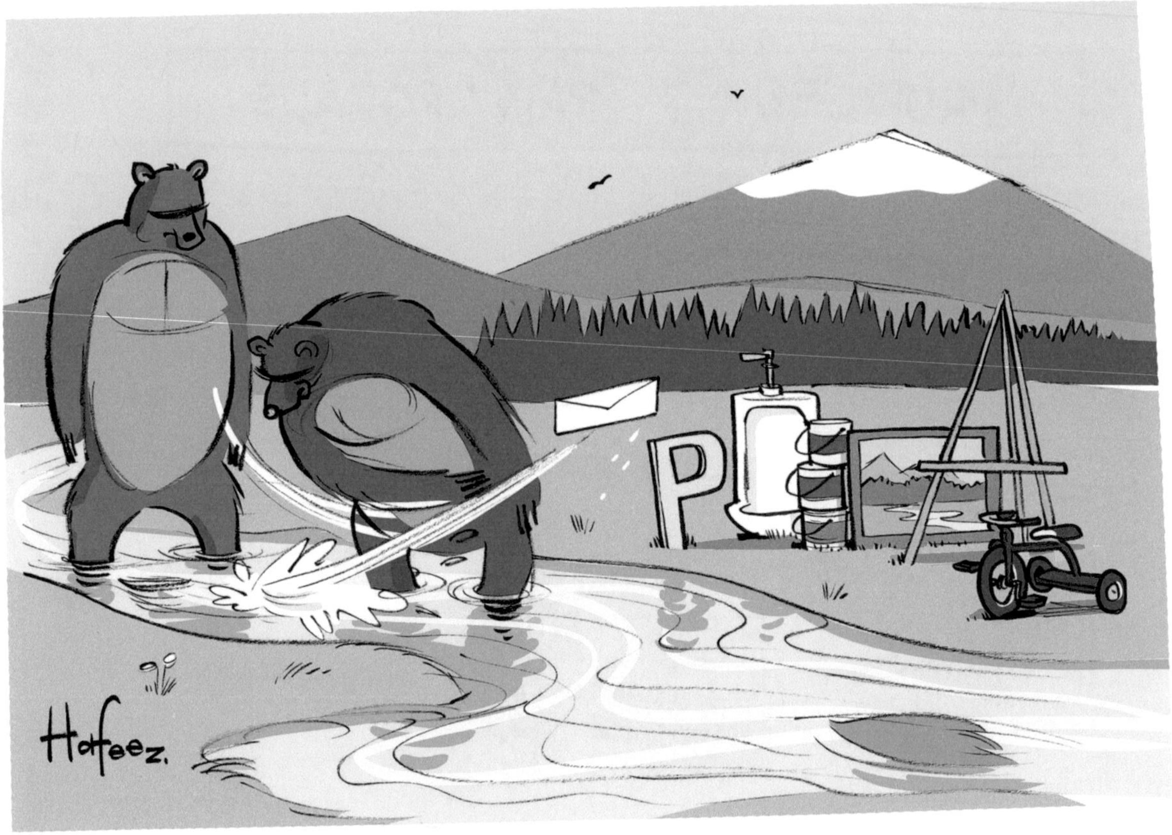
Hafeez.

"Patience, Frank—this is a stream of consciousness."

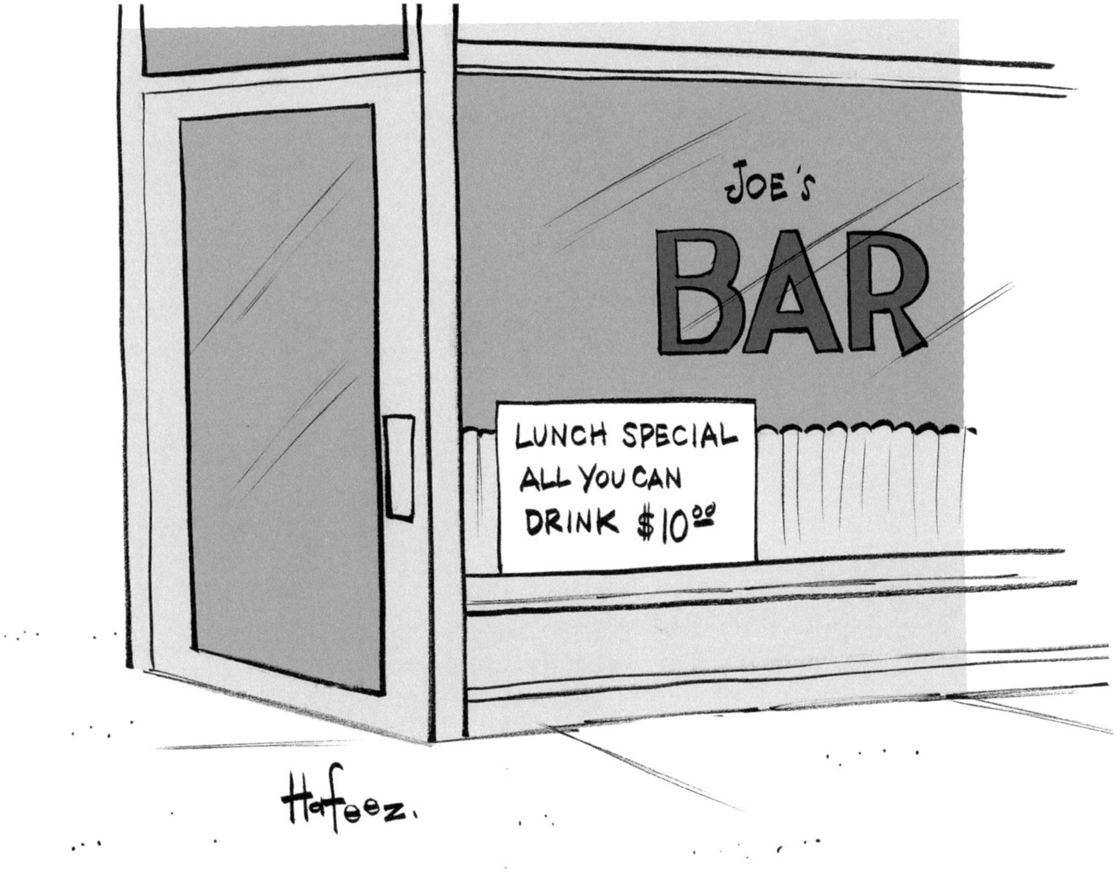
JOE'S
BAR
LUNCH SPECIAL
ALL YOU CAN
DRINK $10.00
Hafeez.

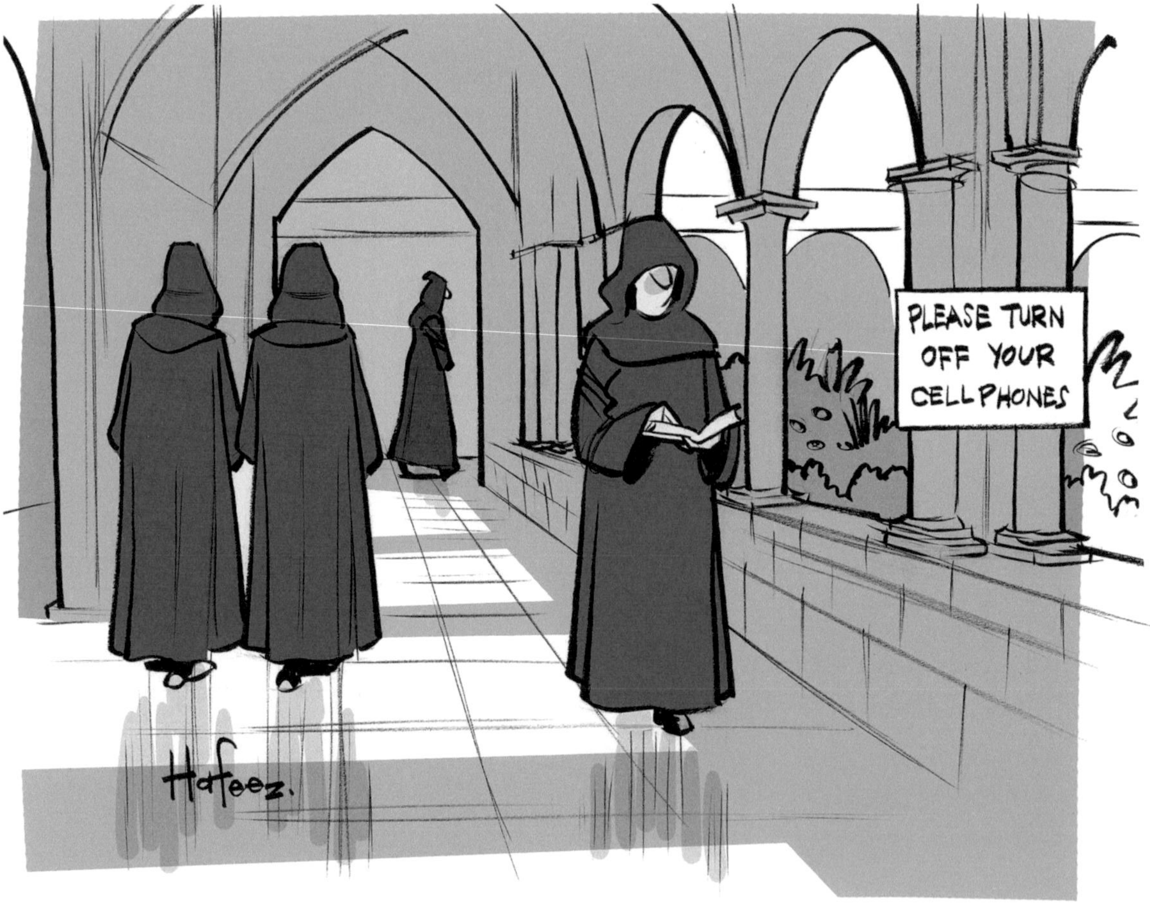
PLEASE TURN
OFF YOUR
CELLPHONES
Hafeez.

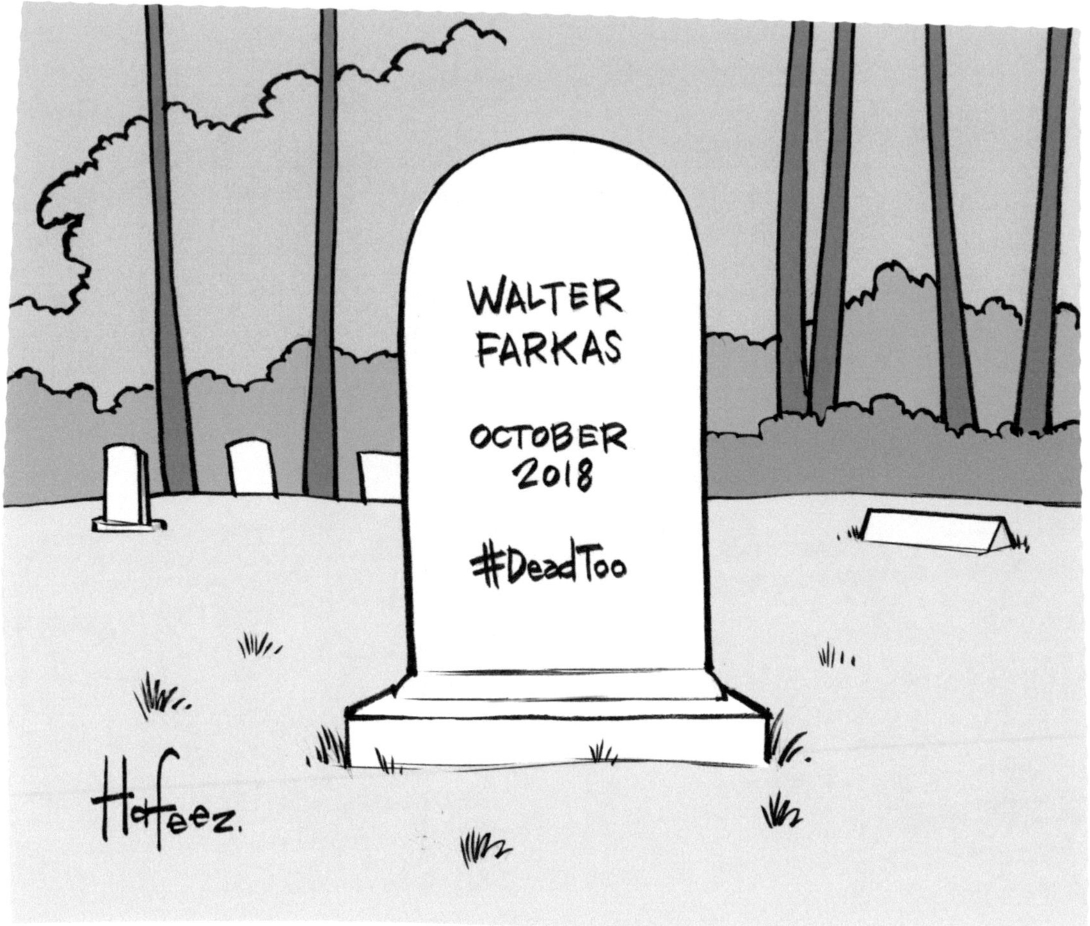
WALTER
FARKAS
OCTOBER
2018
#DeadToo
Hafeez.

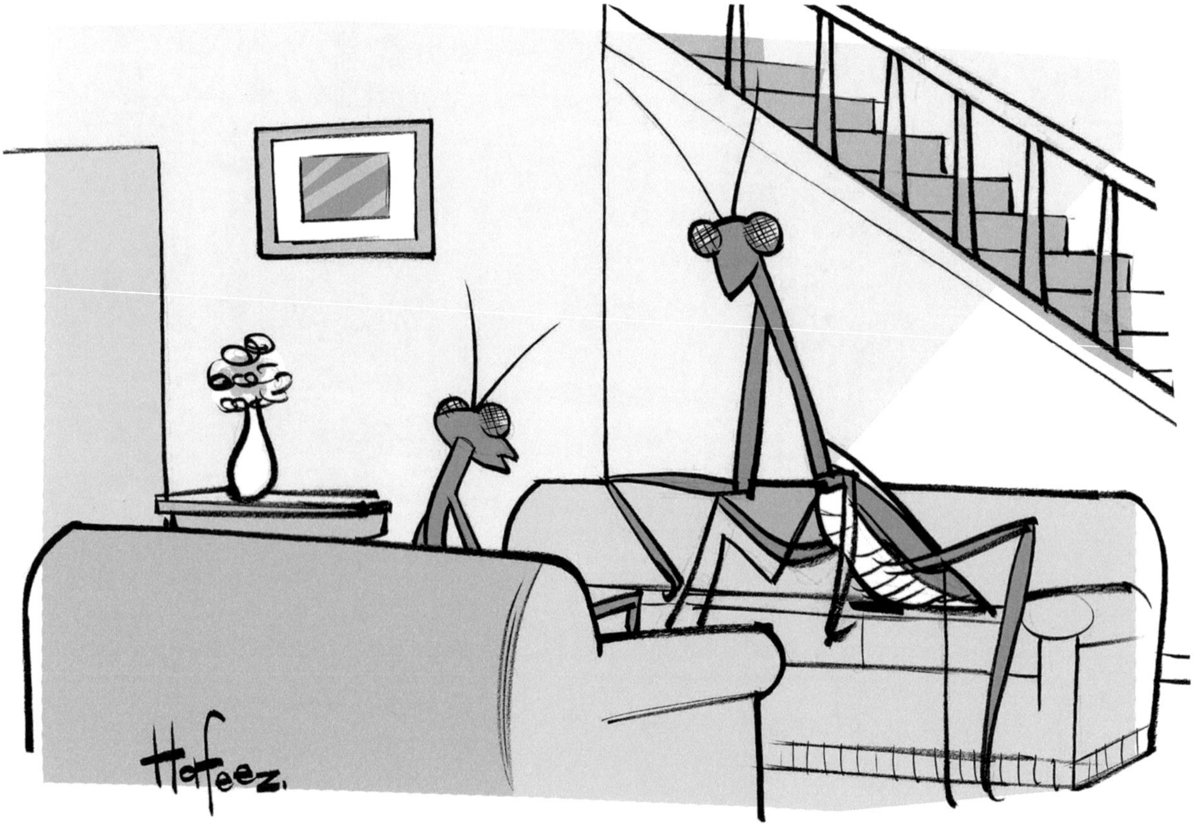
Hafeez.

"You mean Dad's not really in the Peace Corps?"

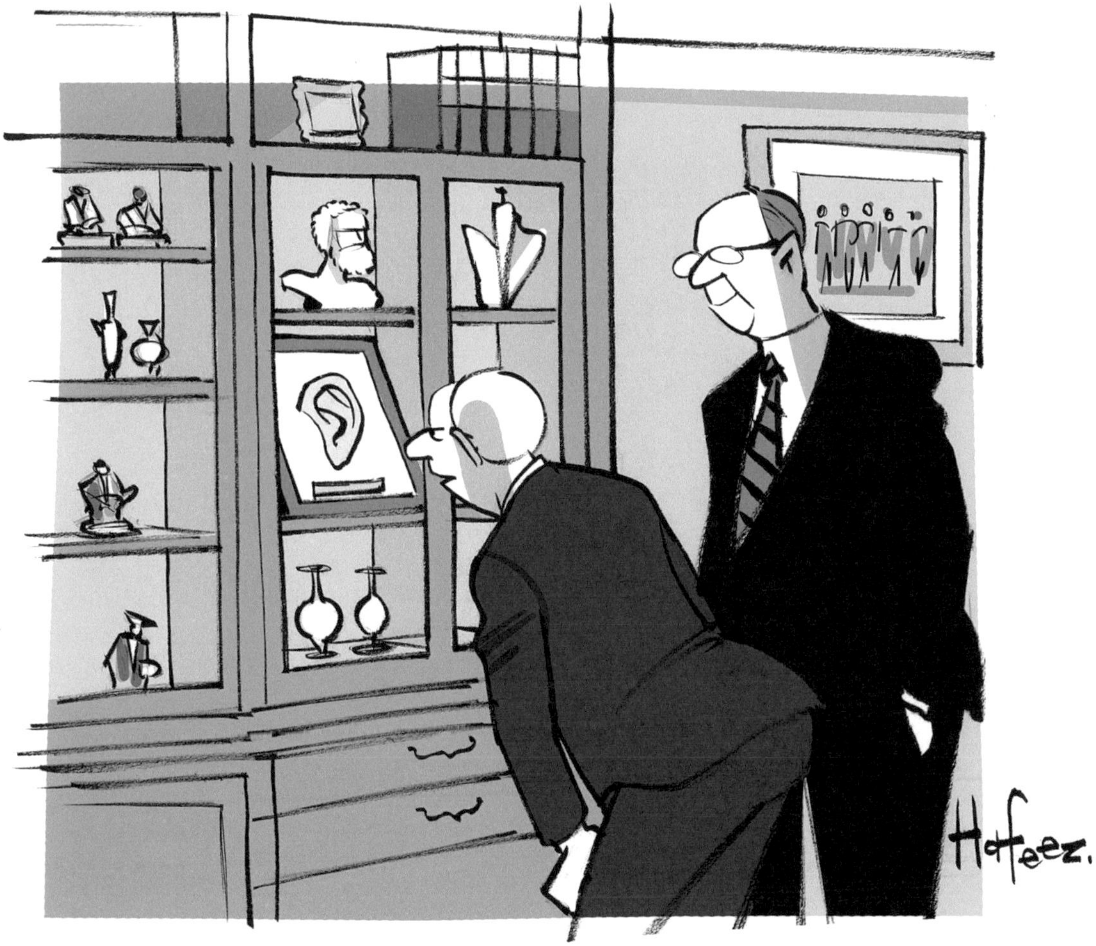
Hafeez.

"I see you still have the President's ear."

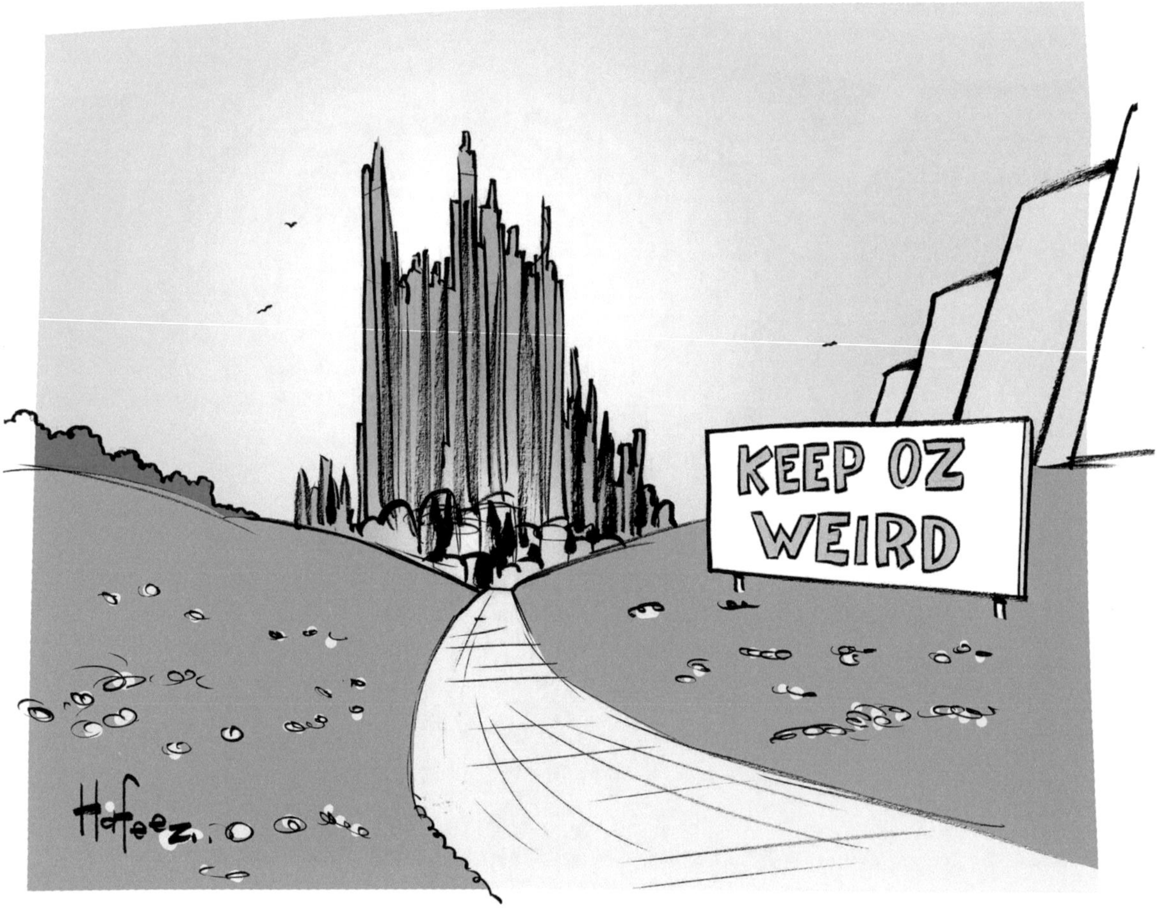
KEEP OZ
WEIRD
Hafeez

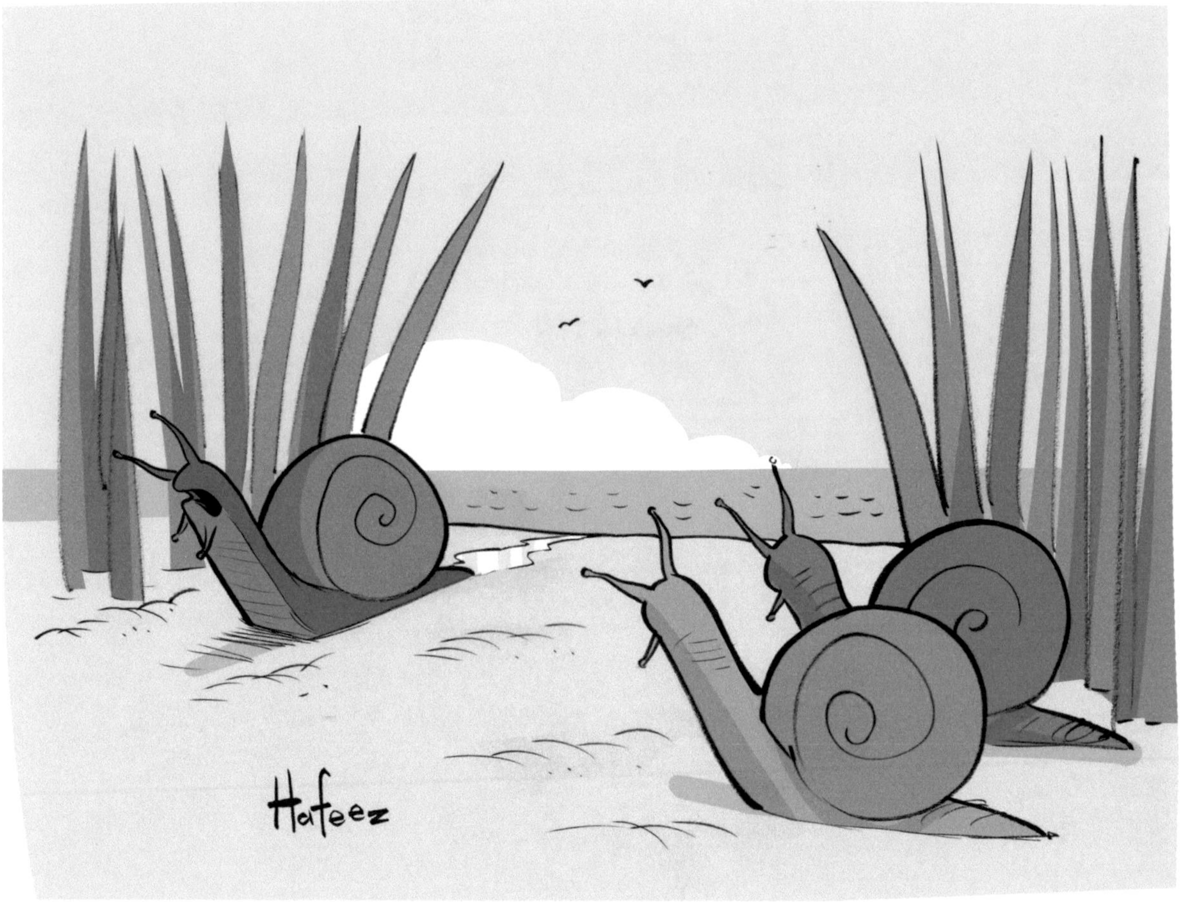
Hafeez

"Run for your lives! The sea is rising at a rate of about 1 foot per century!!"

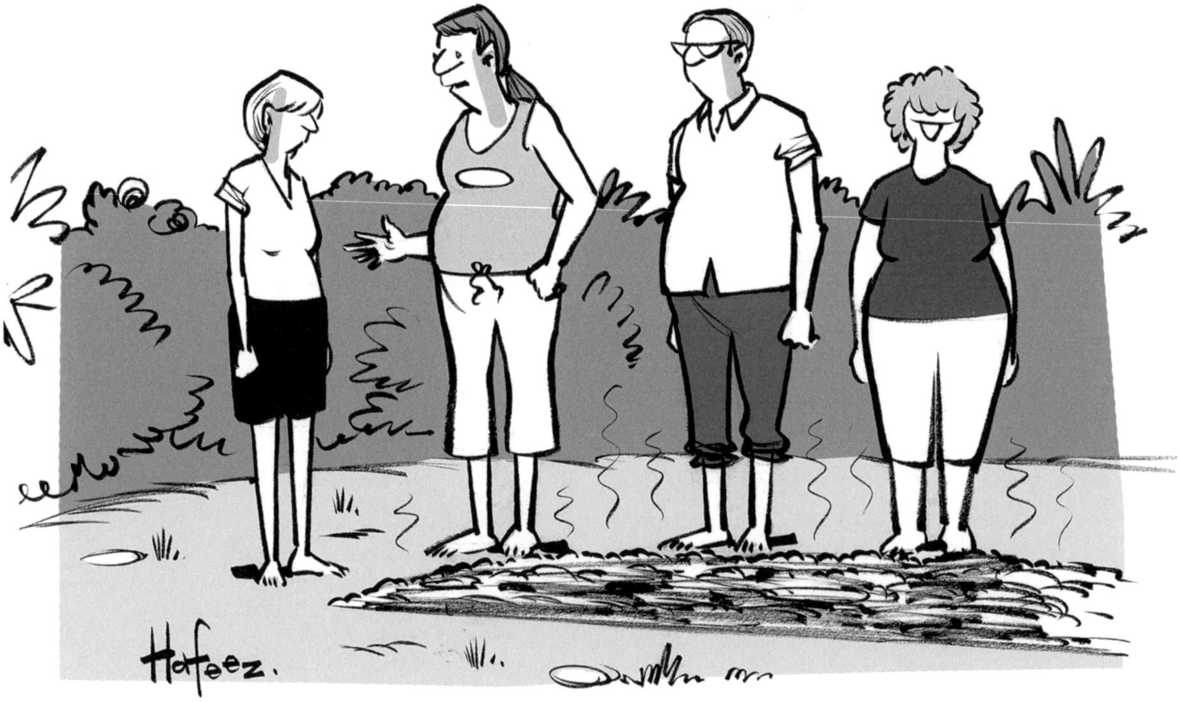
Hafeez.

"Think of it this way—if you can shop for an affordable health care plan, you can walk over a bed of hot coals."

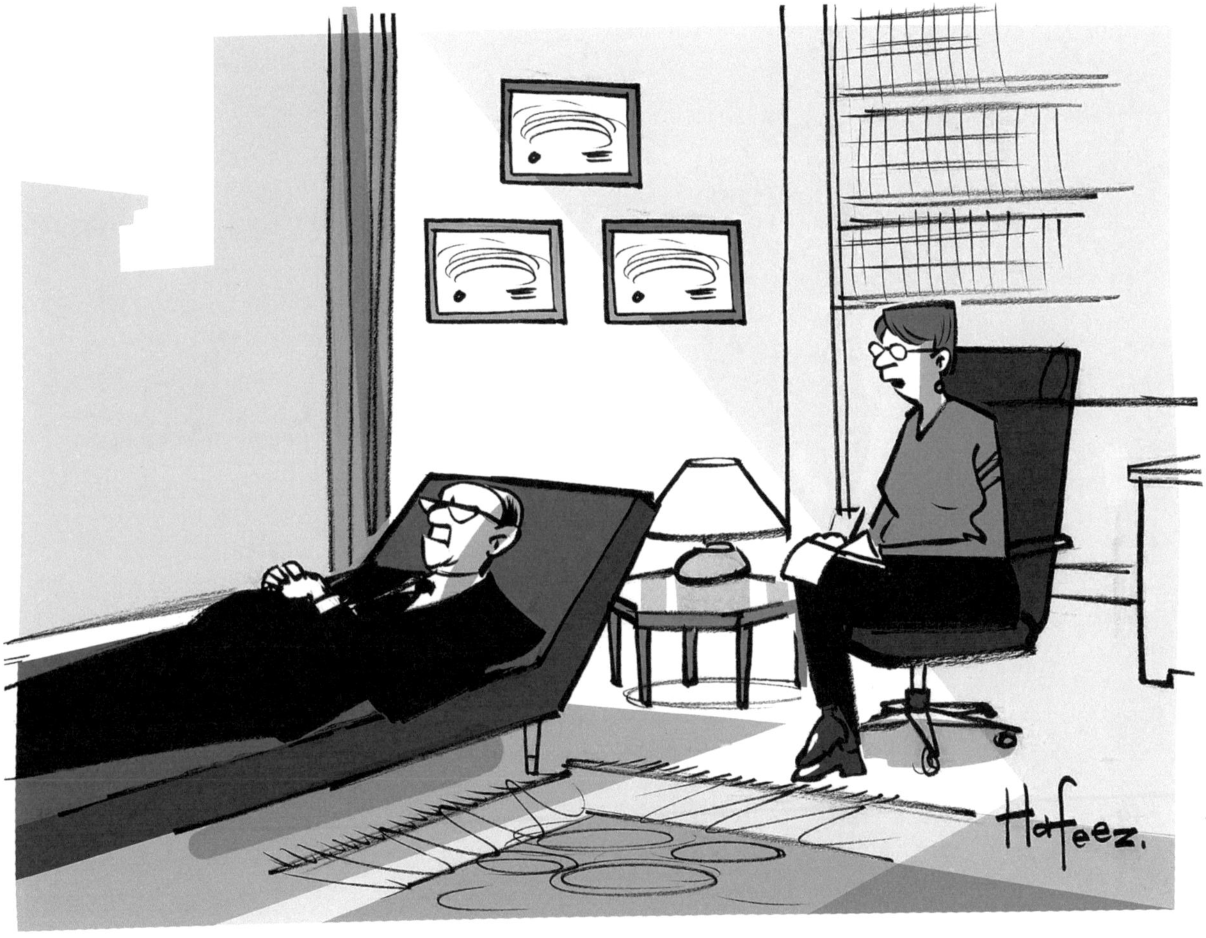
Hafeez.

"Avoidance is a strategy we use to deal with fear, Mr. Farkas—or in your case, paying taxes."

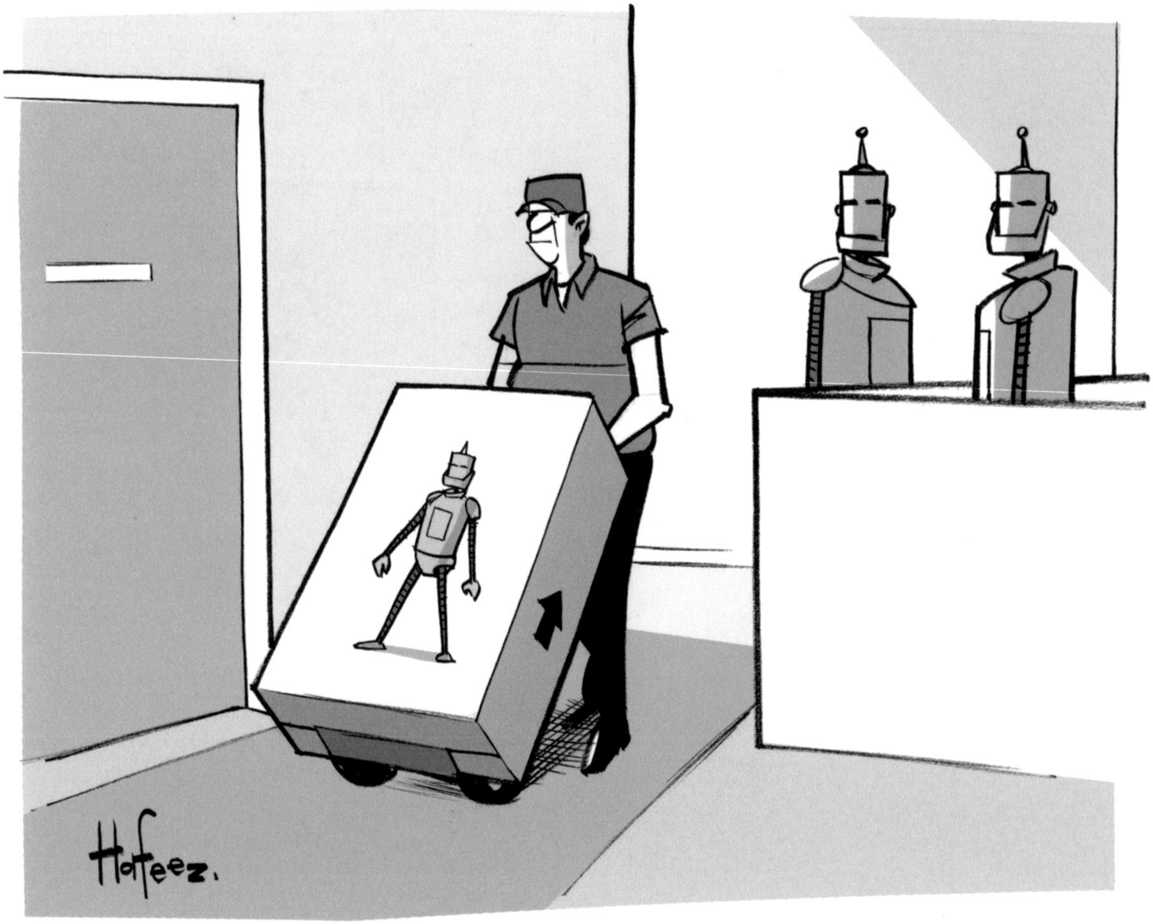
Hafeez.

"Who's the new guy?"

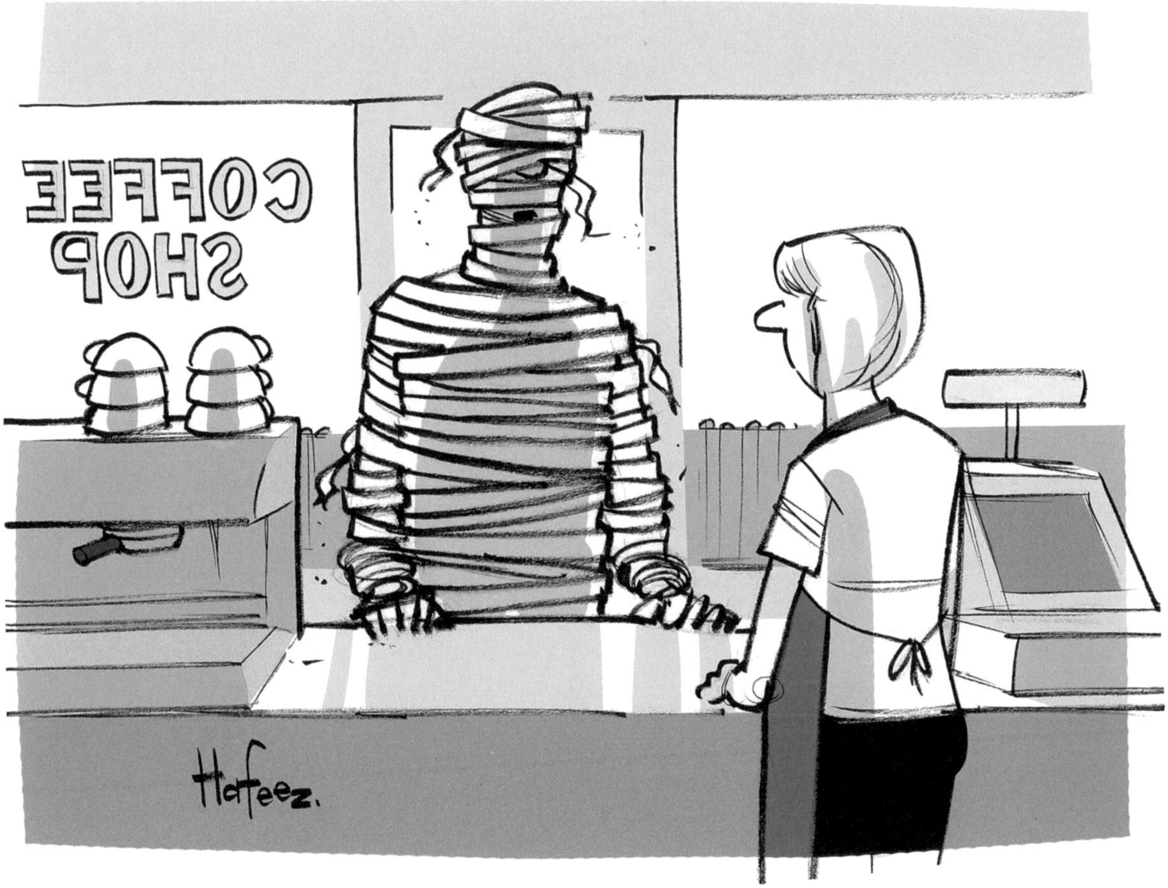
COFFEE
SHOP
Hafeez.

"Do you accept cryptocurrency?"

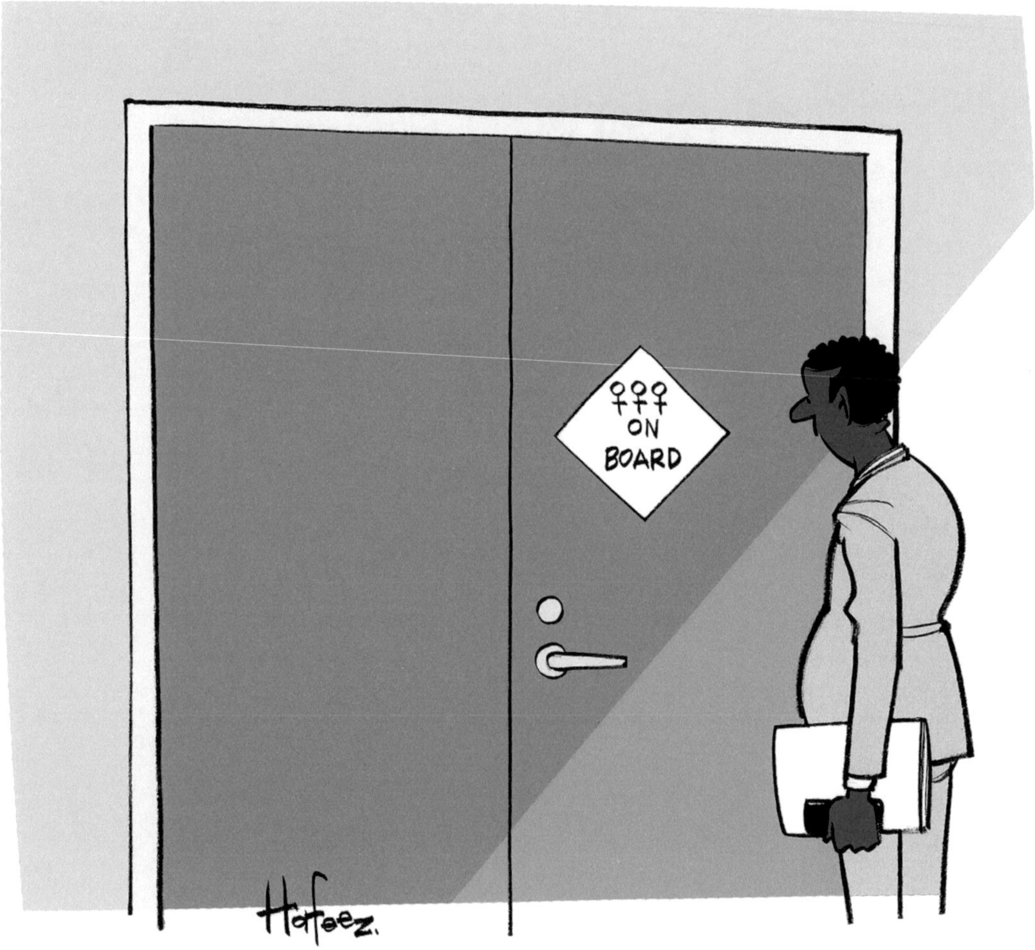
♀♀♀
ON
BOARD
Hafeez.

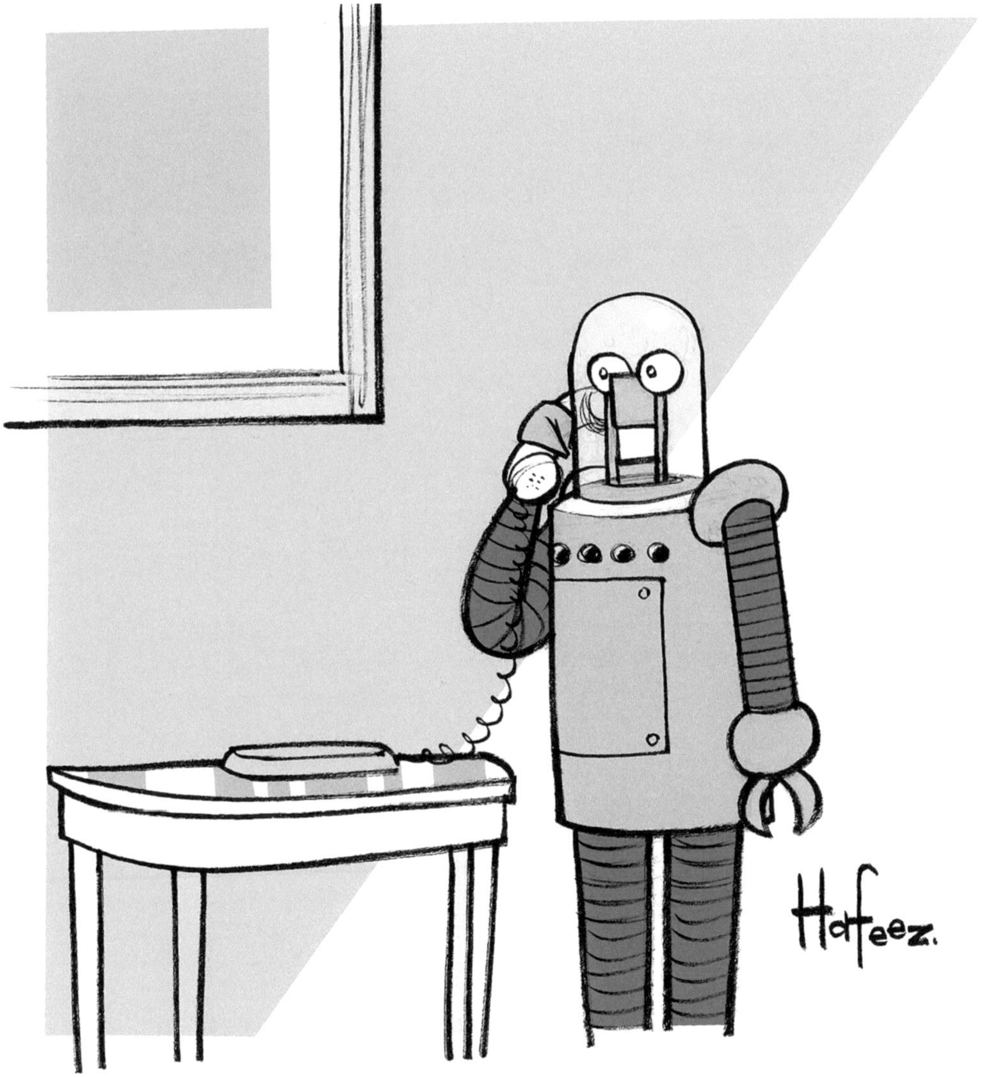
Hafeez.

"Hello, Mr. Burnham? I won't be in today—I have a bad code."

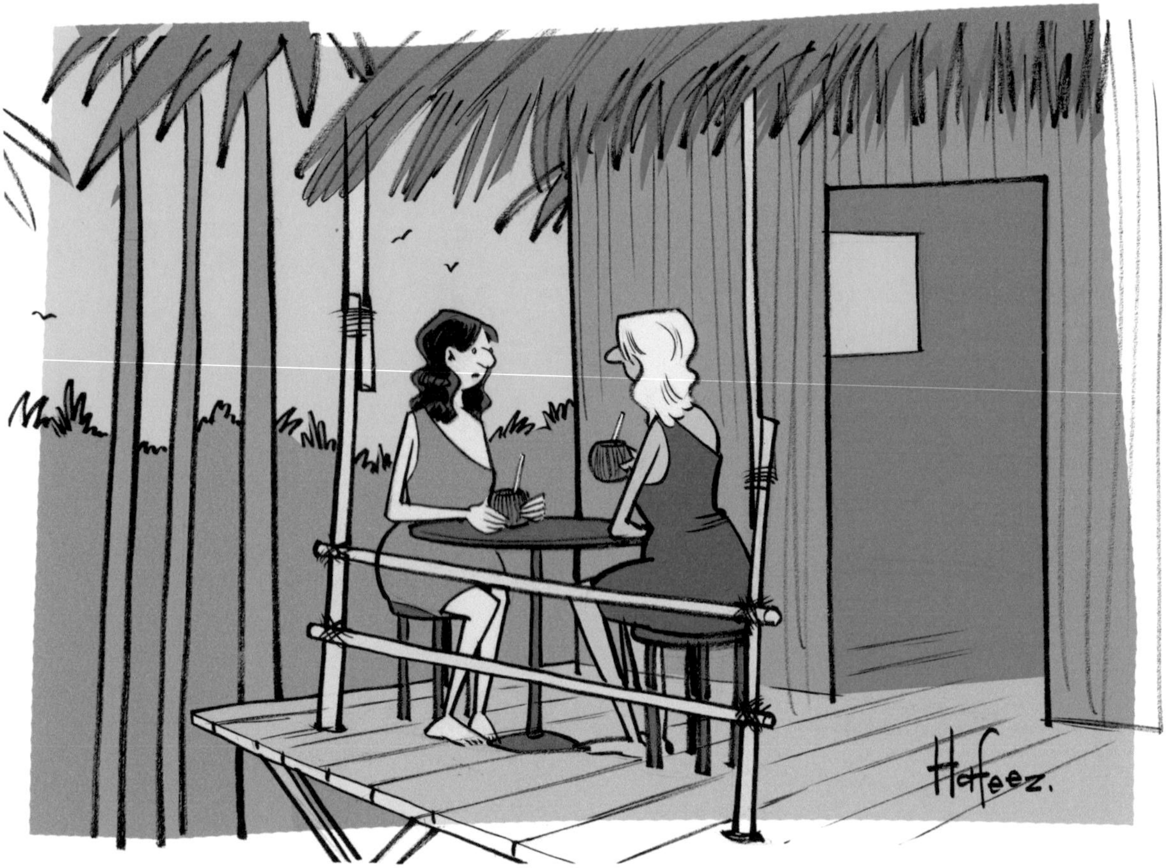
Hafeez.

"Most of the time it's 'Me Tarzan, you Jane', until we get into the bedroom. Then he's all, 'You Tarzan, <u>me</u> Jane'."

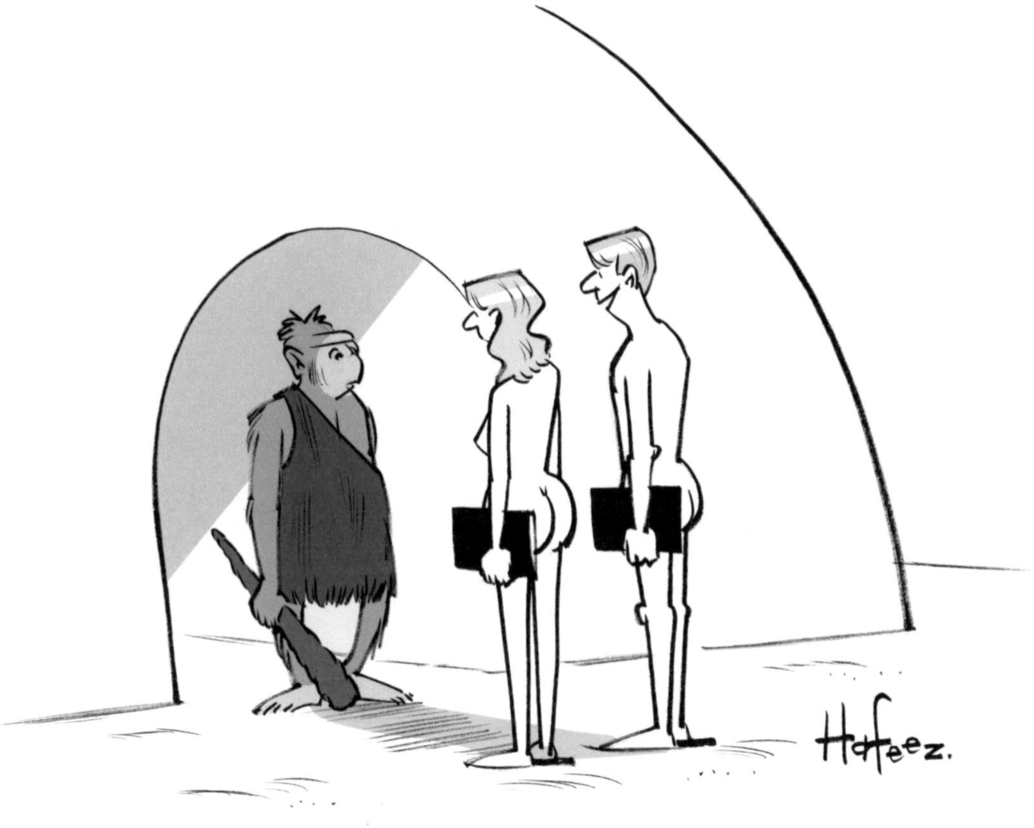
Hafeez.

"Do you have a few minutes to talk about Creation?"

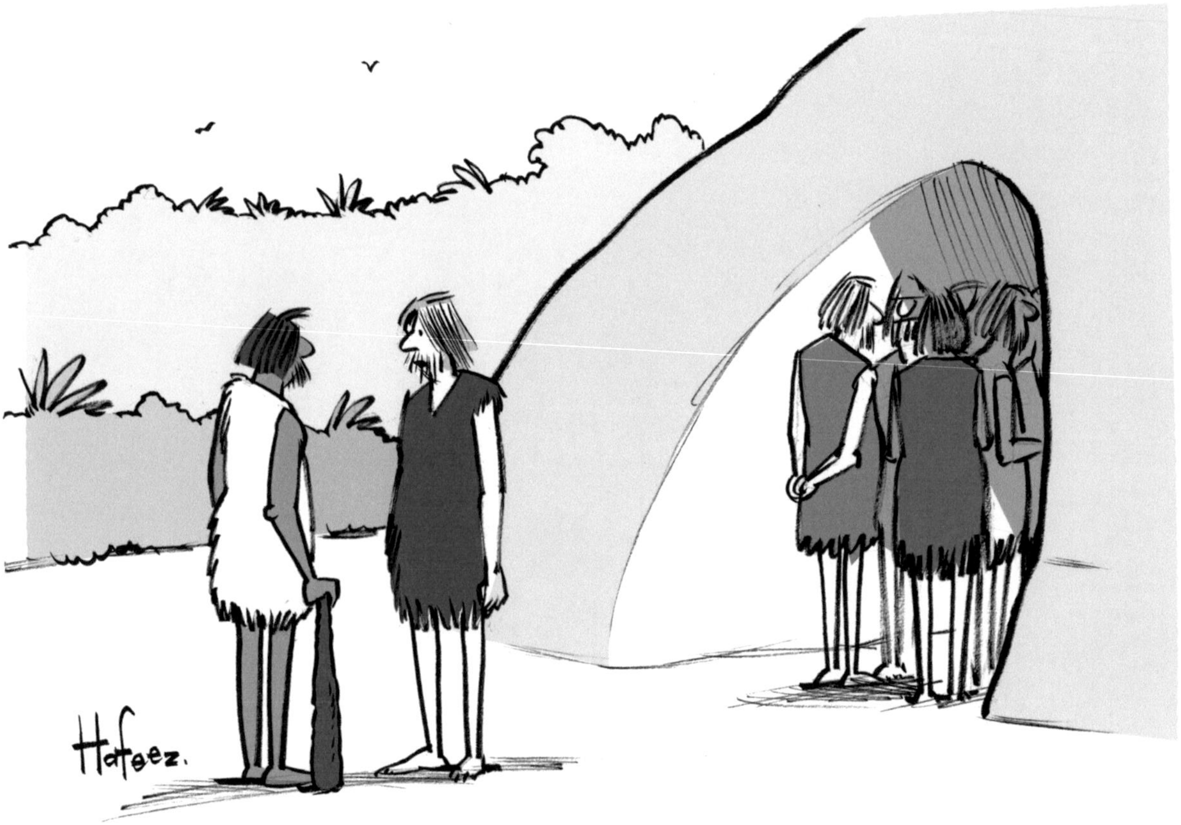
Hafeez.

"It's a tool for power and control—it's called a 'club'."

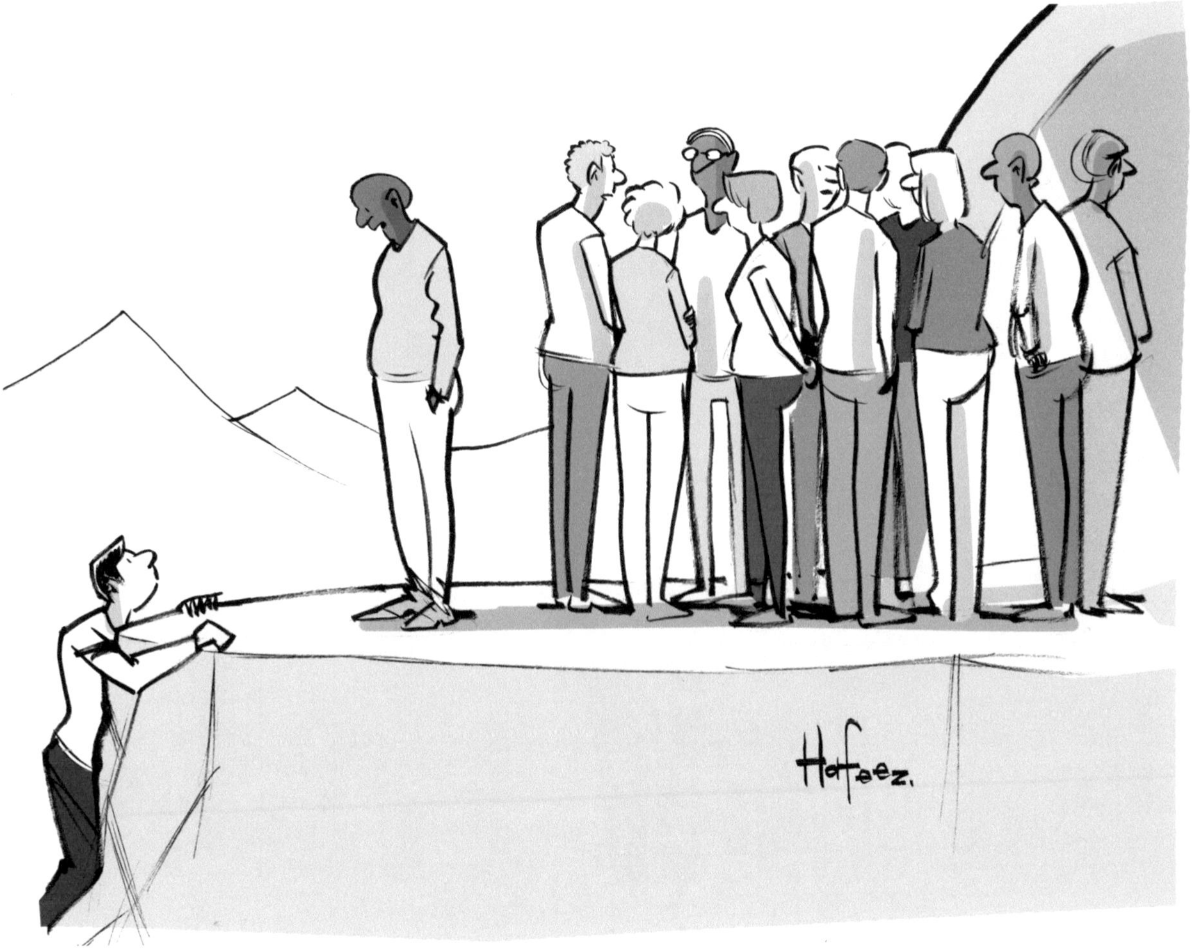
Hafeez.

"Gurus are the next peak over—this is the Wisdom of the Crowd."

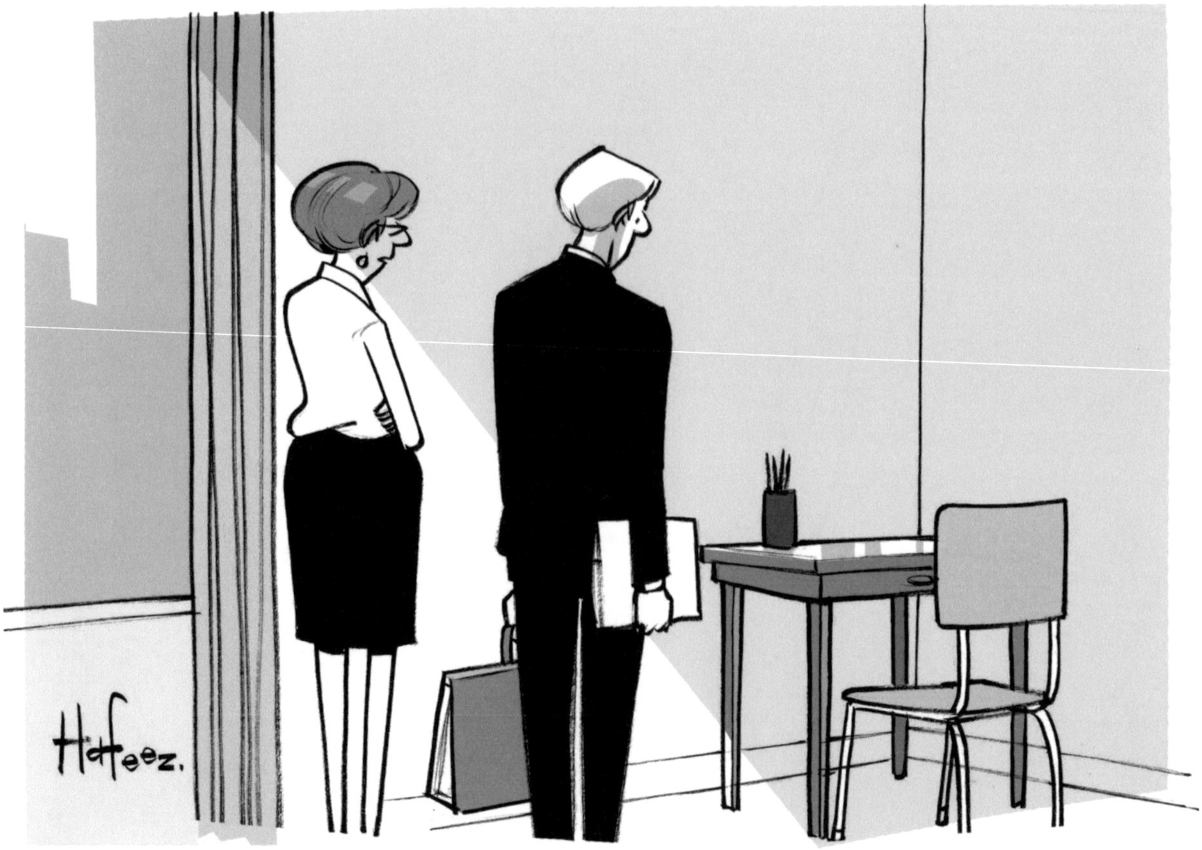
Hafeez.

"Did I say 'corner office'? I meant 'corner of my office'."

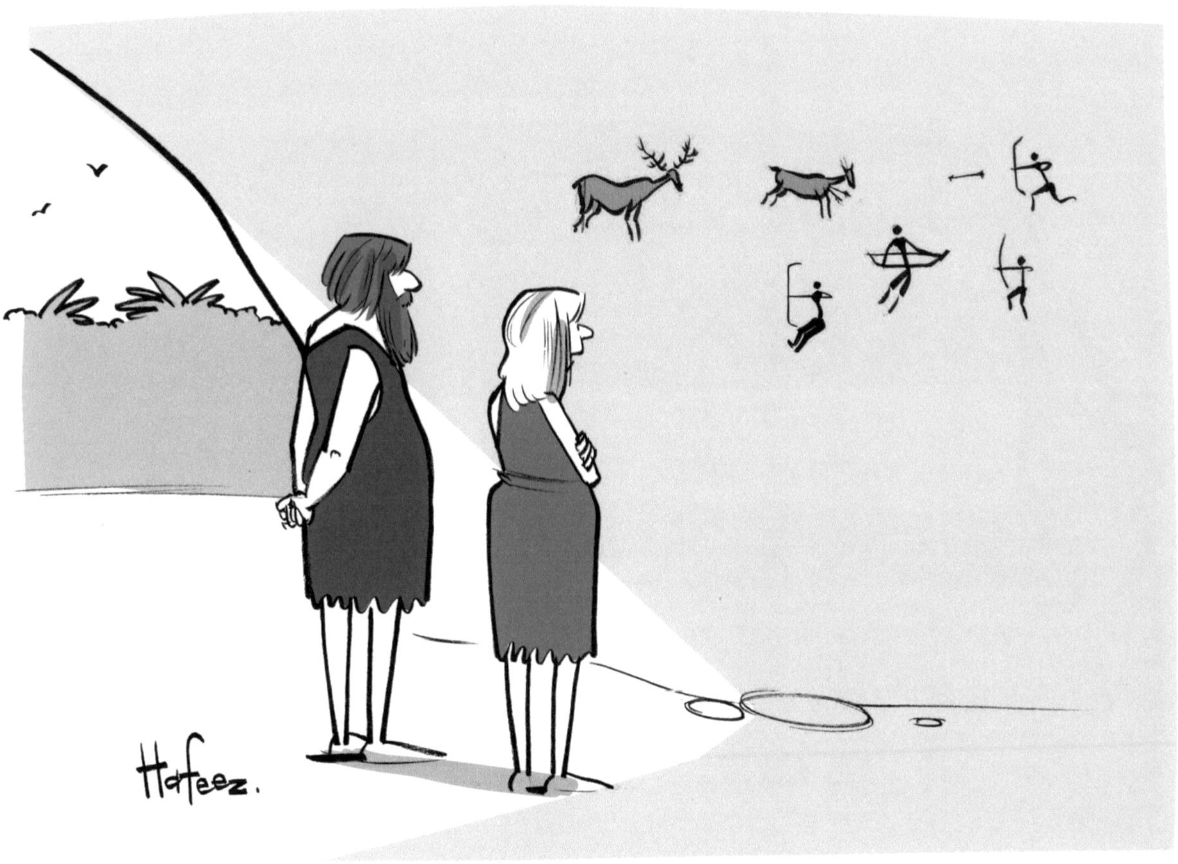
Hafeez.

"There's no privacy anymore."

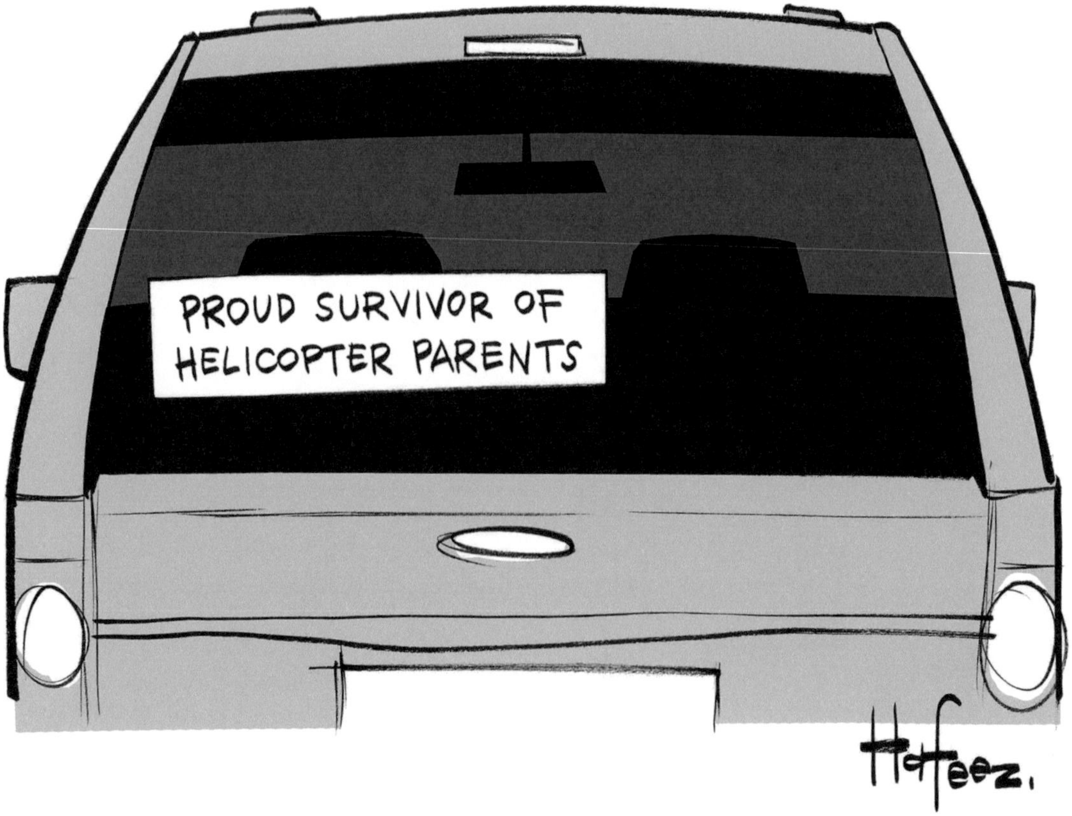
PROUD SURVIVOR OF
HELICOPTER PARENTS
Hafeez.

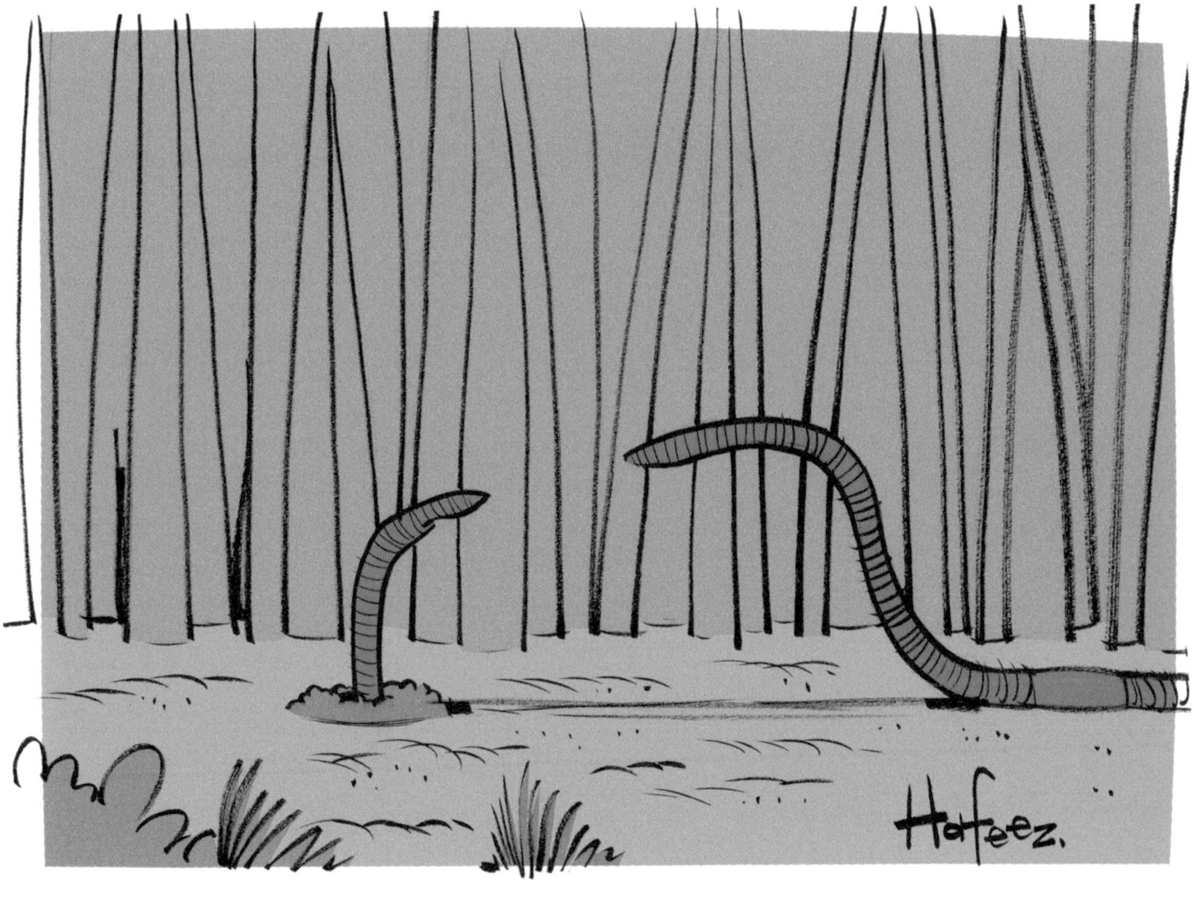
Hafeez.

"I make a point of sleeping in."

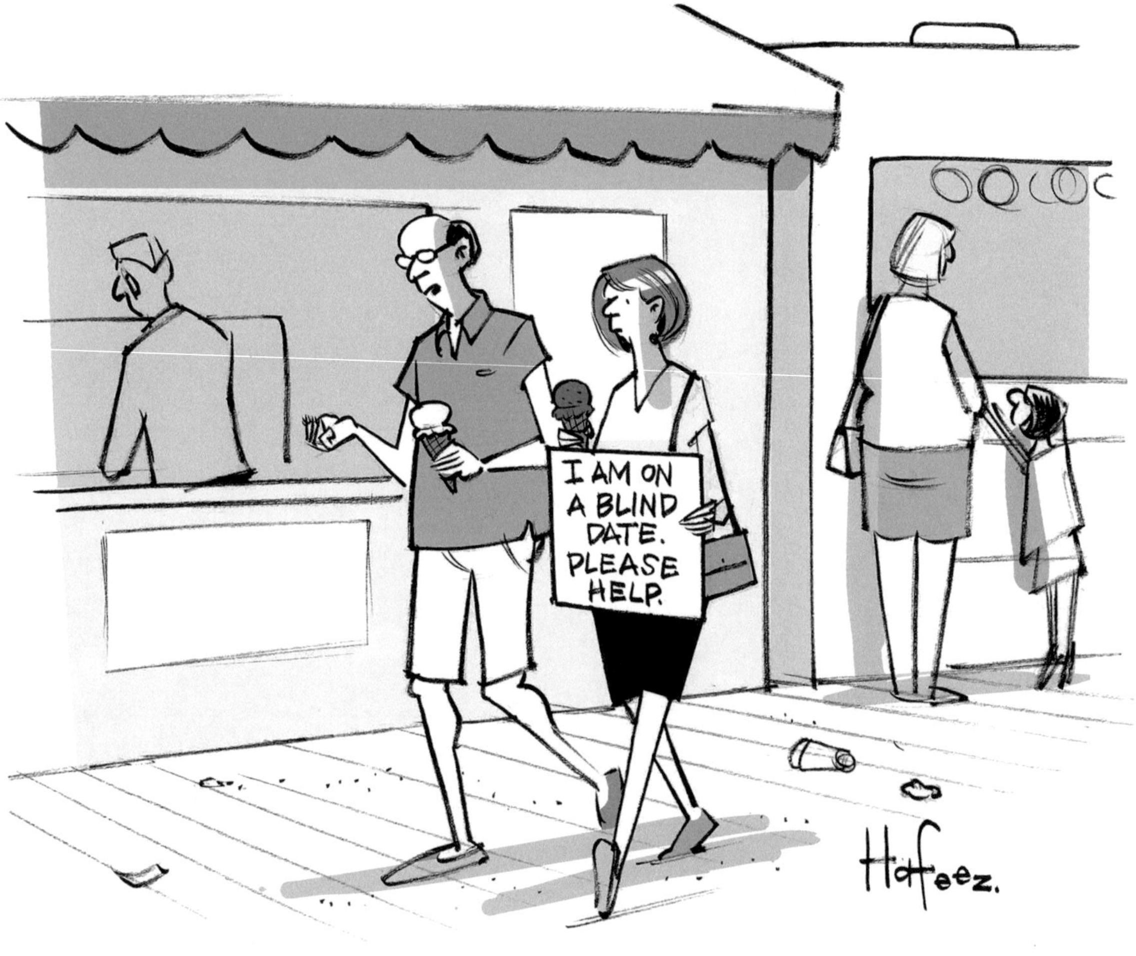
I AM ON A BLIND DATE. PLEASE HELP.
Hafeez.

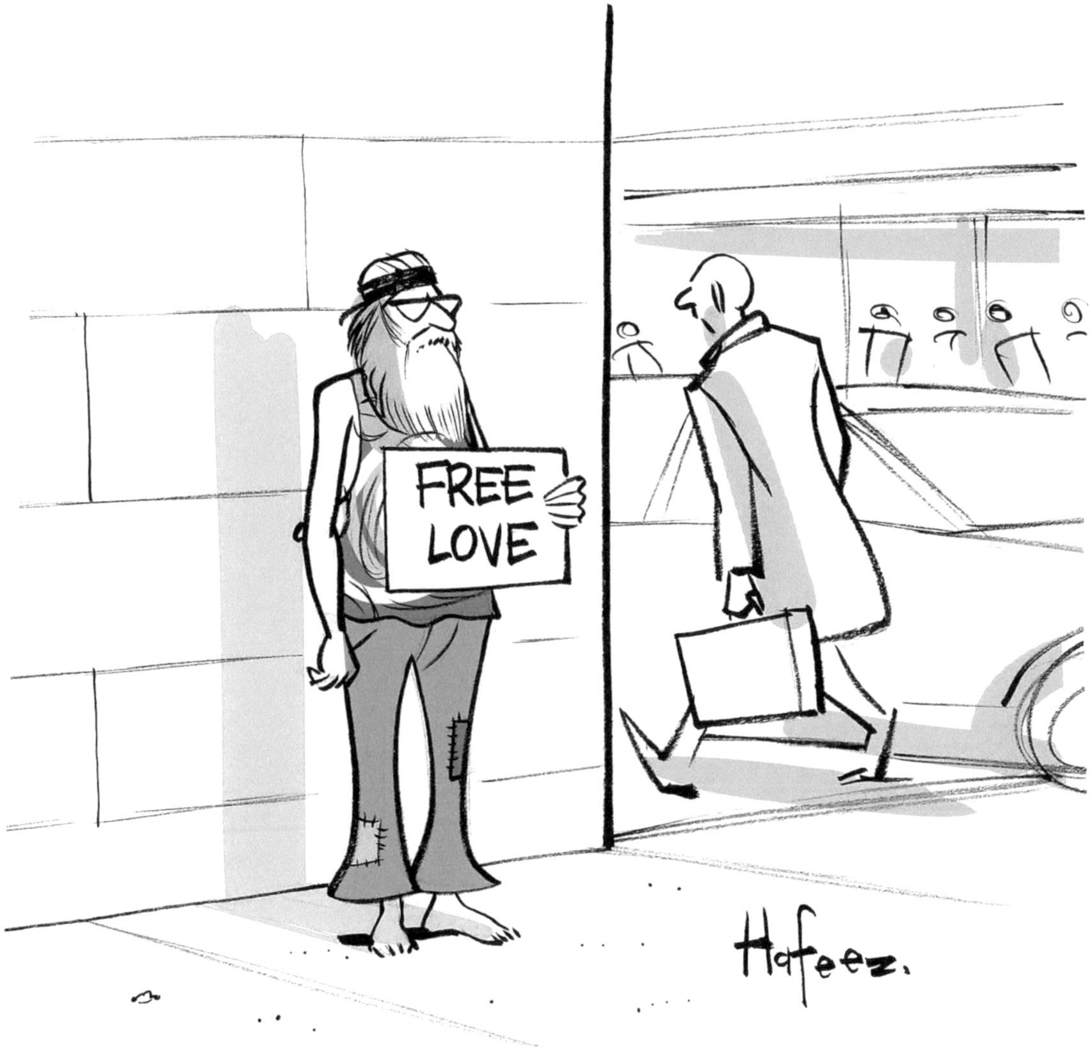
FREE
LOVE
Hafeez.

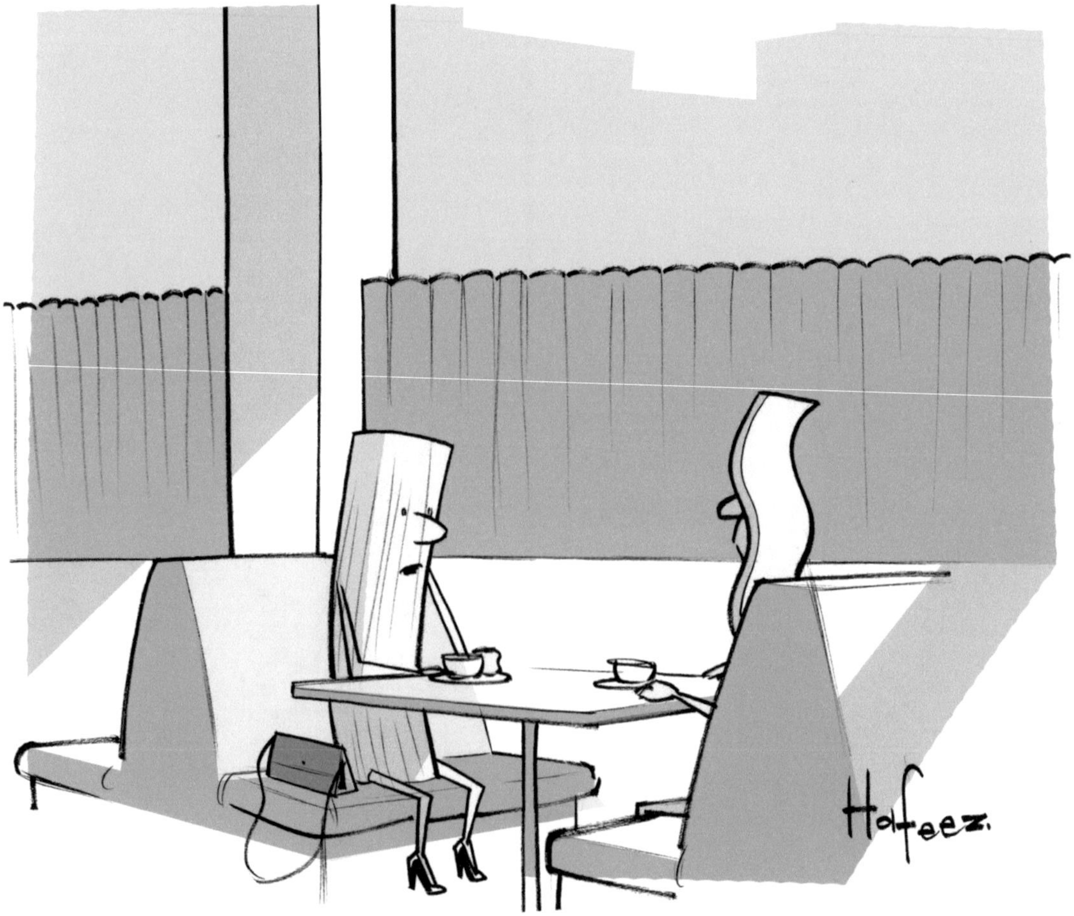
Hafeez.

"The thing is, Jeremy—I'm al dente and you're a wet noodle."

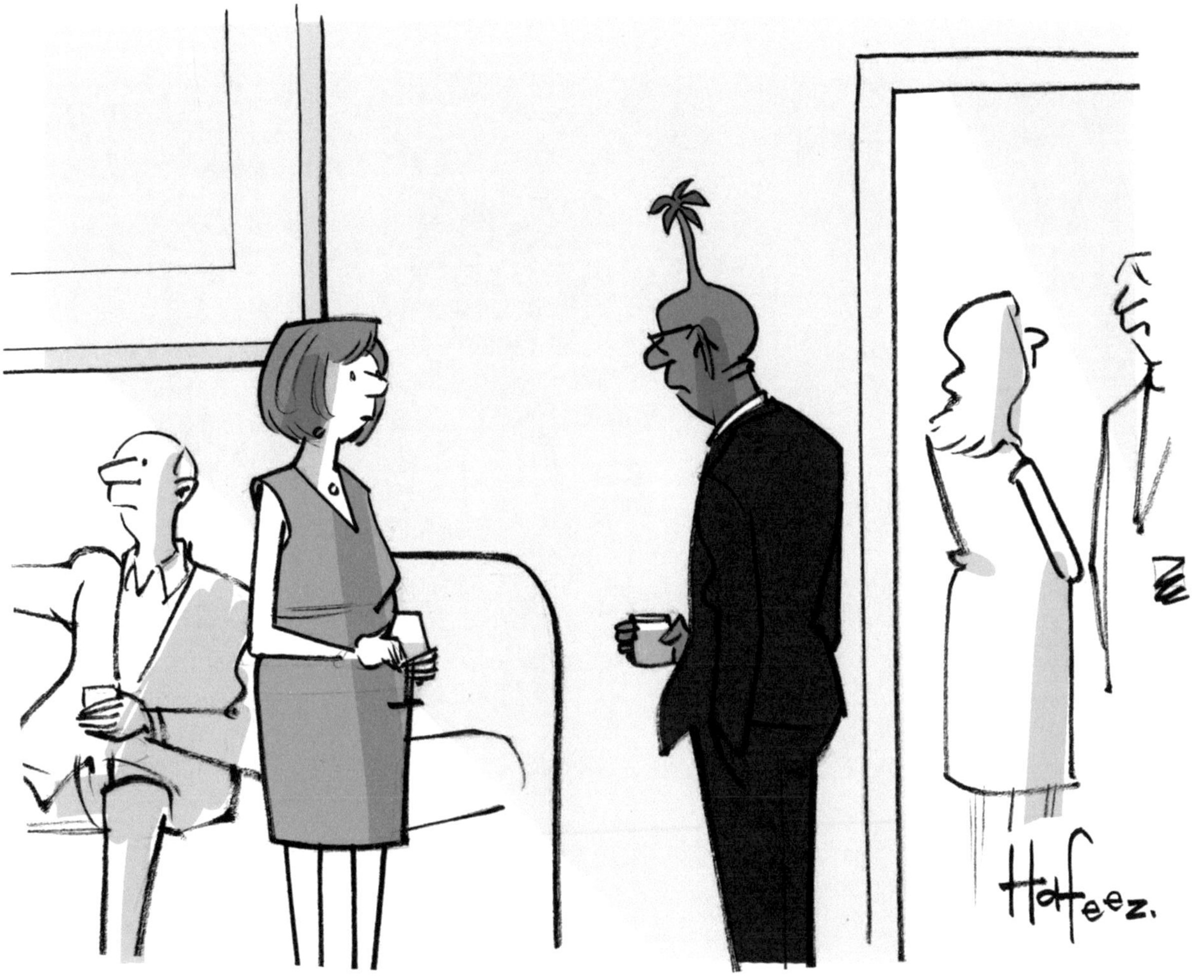
Hafeez.

"No man is an island, that's true. But I come pretty close."

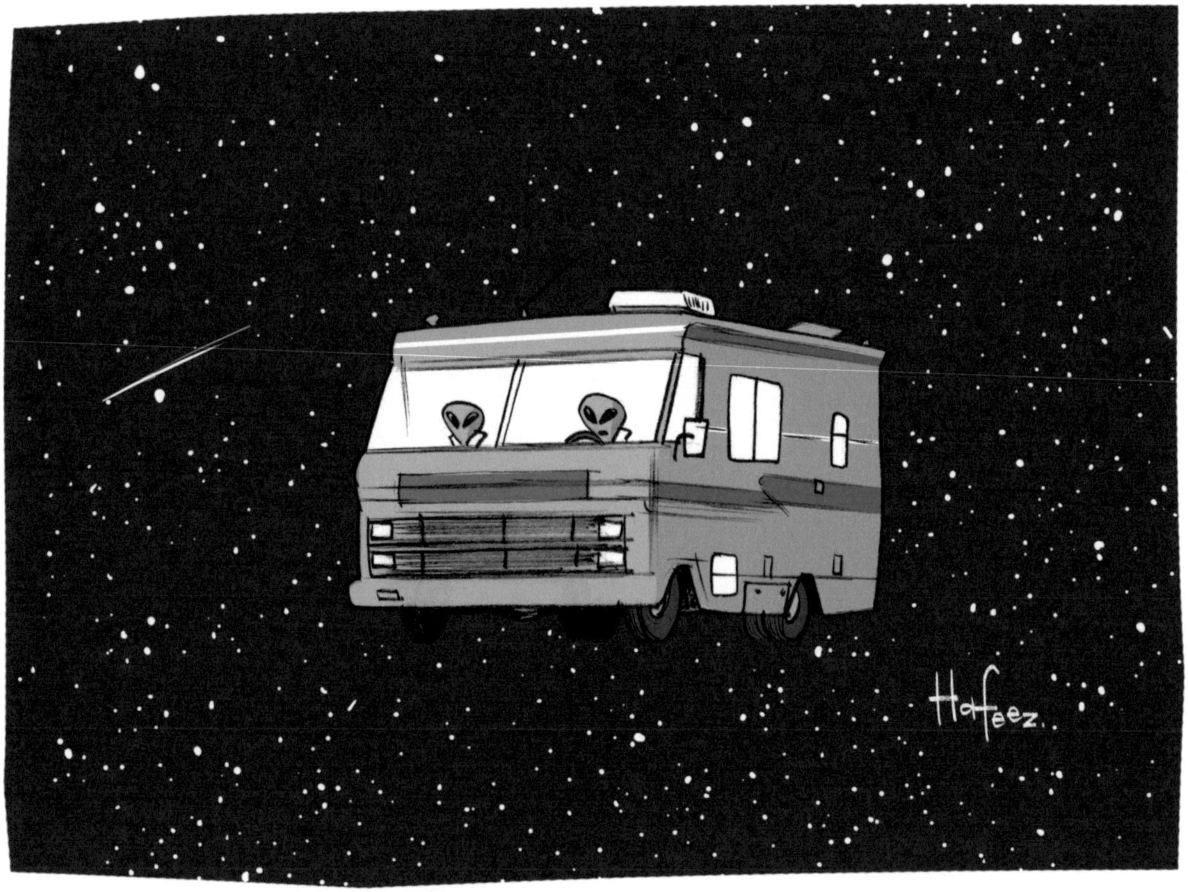
Hafeez.

"Hang on—I'm going to make the jump to 90 m.p.h."

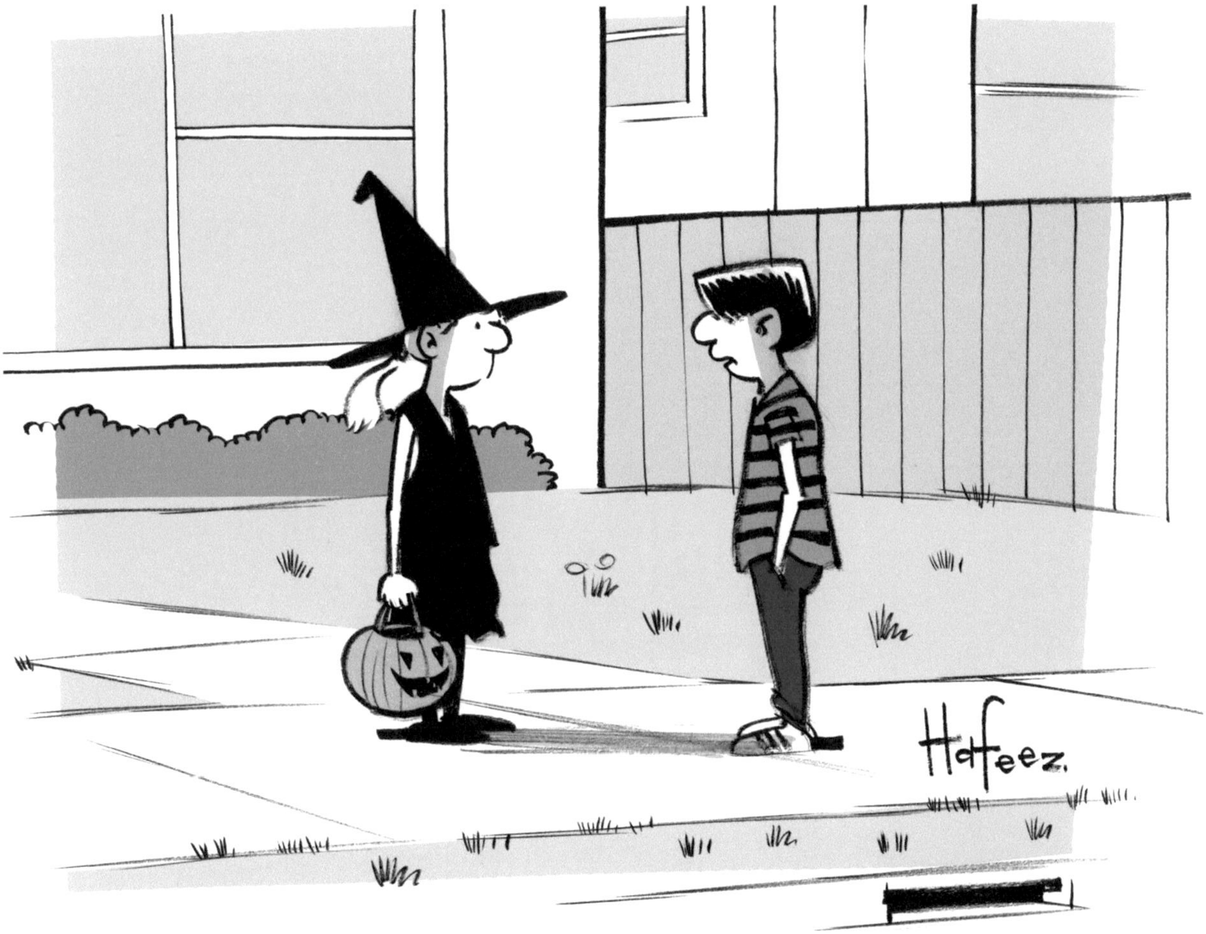
Hafeez.

"A haunted house is nothing. My Mom took me to a lecture on the effects of sugar."

LEVEL 1
LEVEL 2
LEVEL 3
LEVEL 4
LEVEL 5
LEVEL 6
LEVEL 7
FOOD STORAGE & MATING
NURSERIES & WORKER HOUSING
EXEC OFFICES & LABORATORIES
MIND CONTROL EXPERIMENTS
ALIEN HOUSING – THE GREYS
GENETIC EXPERIMENTS
CRYOGENICS
TO INNER EARTH
TO LOS ALAMOS
QUEEN
Hafeez.

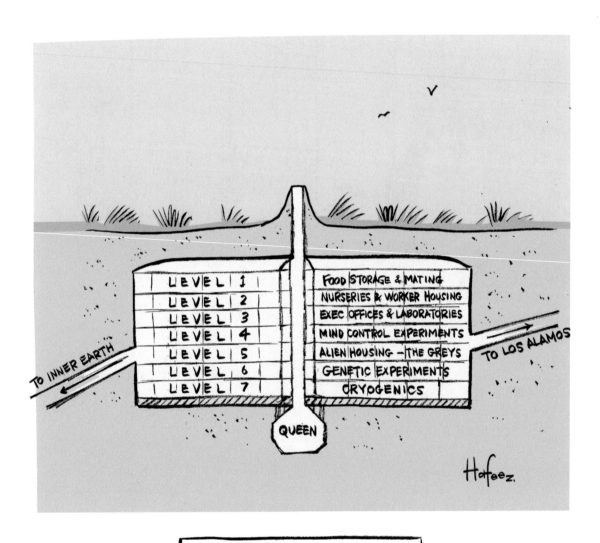

CONSPIRACY ANTS

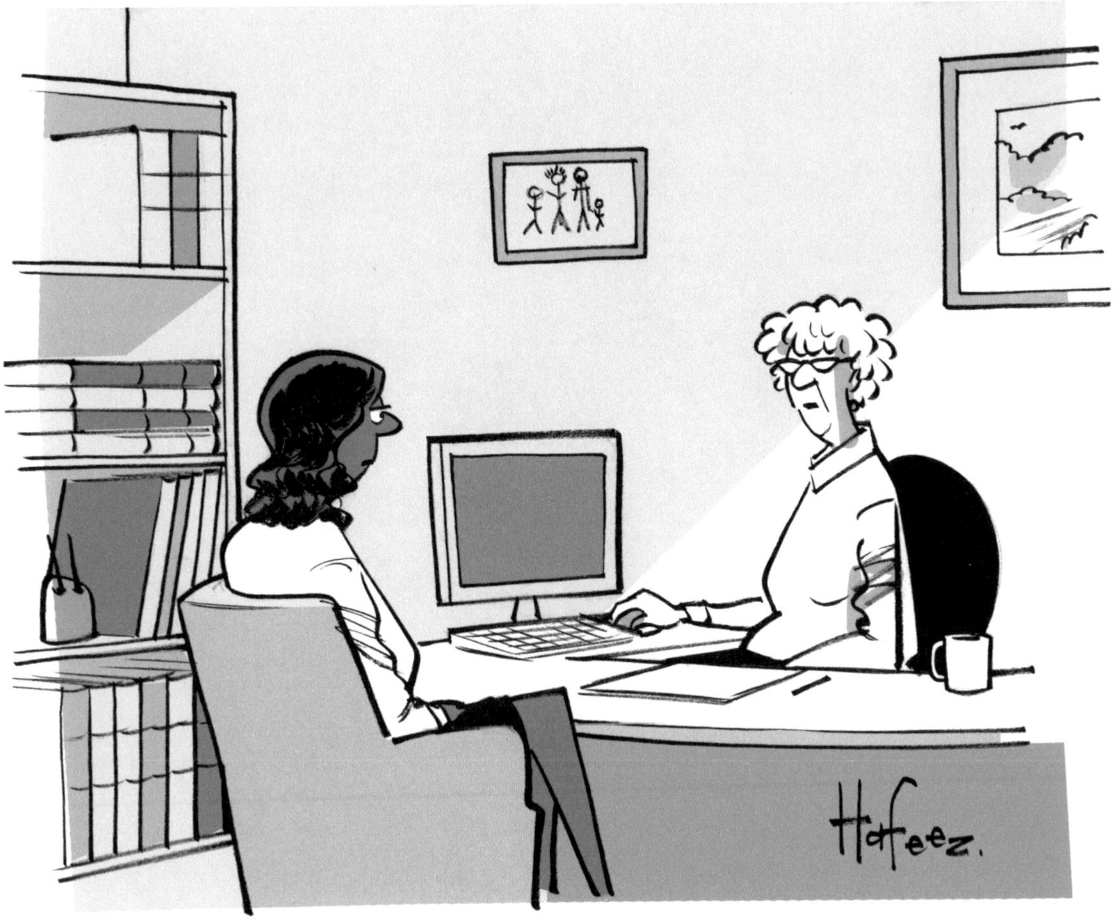
Hafeez.

"Only the most egregious offence is grounds for dismissal—like embezzlement, lying to your boss, or having a family."

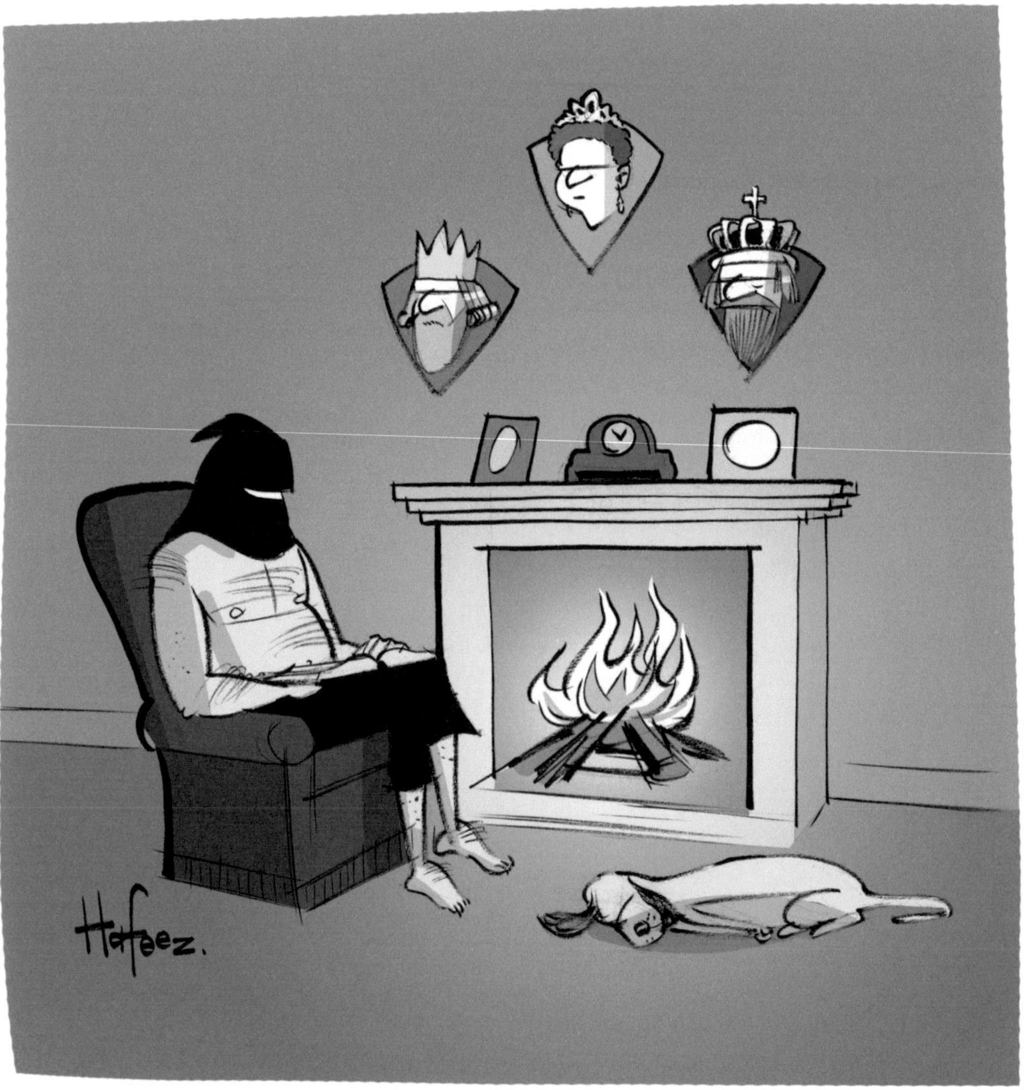
Hafeez.

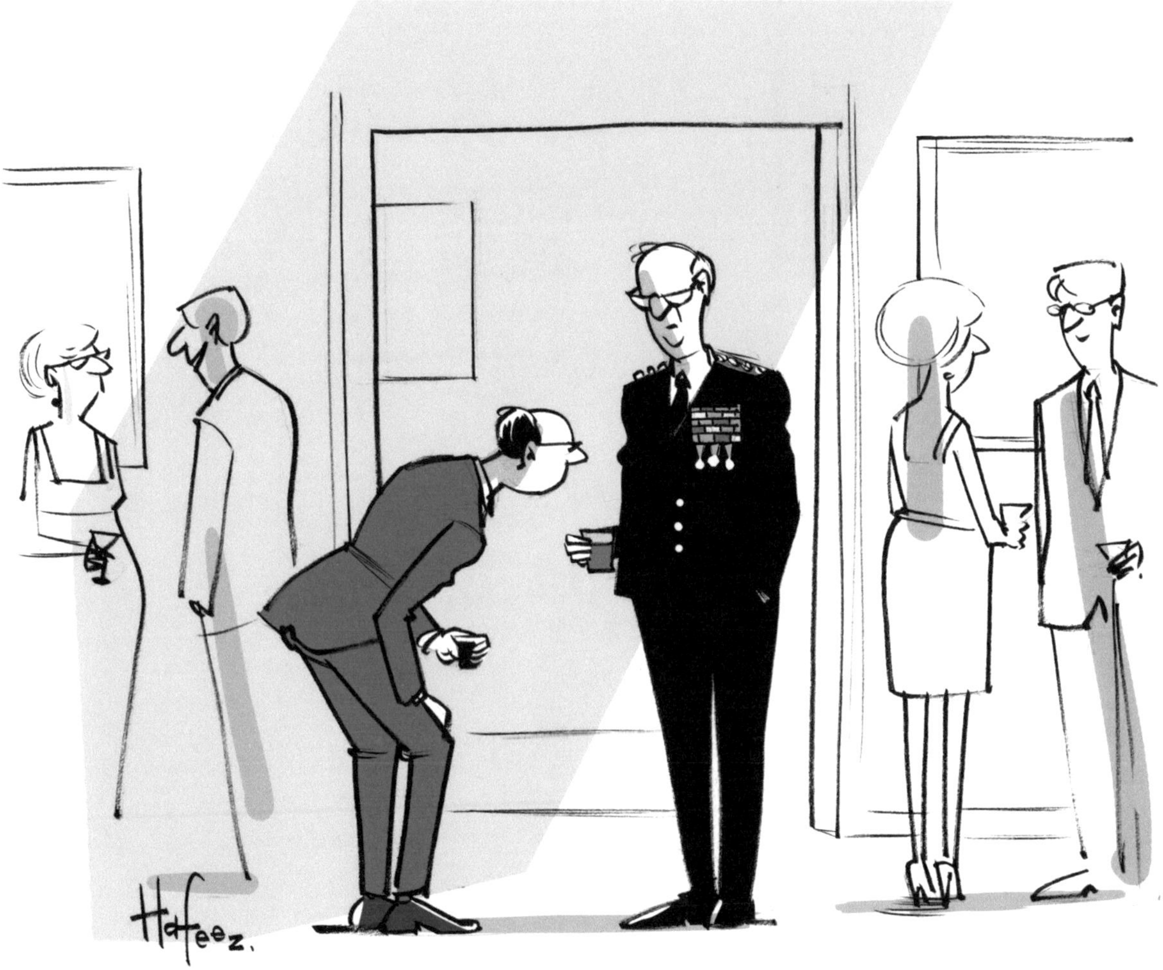
Hafeez.

"That's my kidney stone."

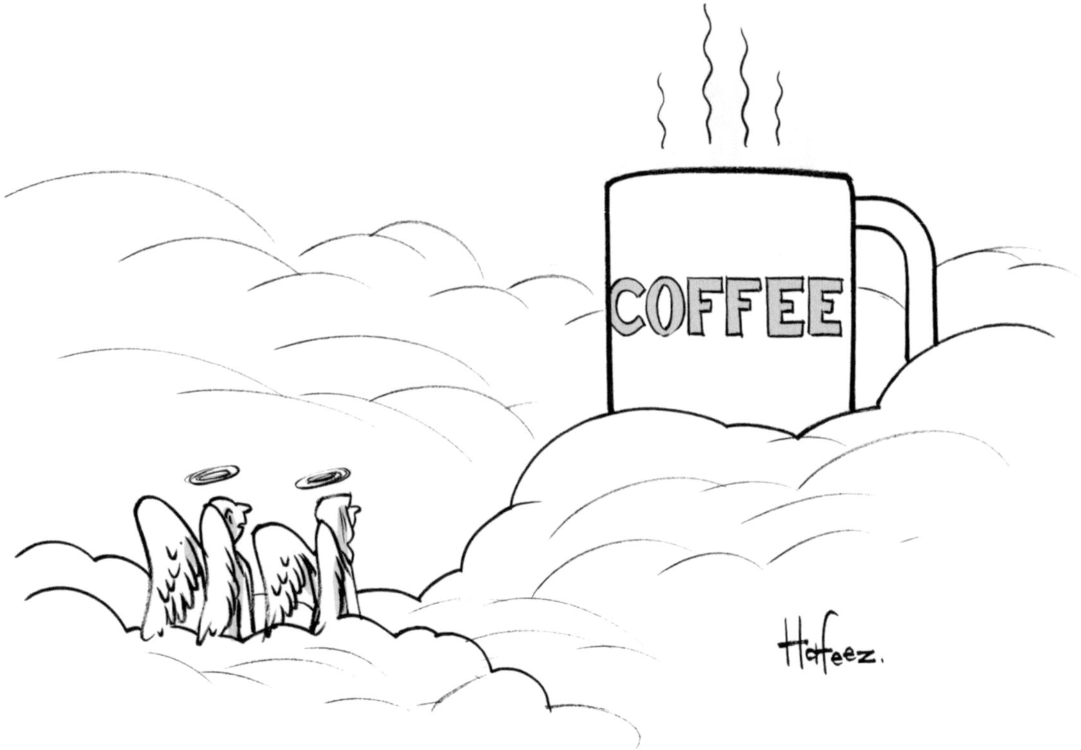
COFFEE
Hafeez.

"It's not what I was expecting."

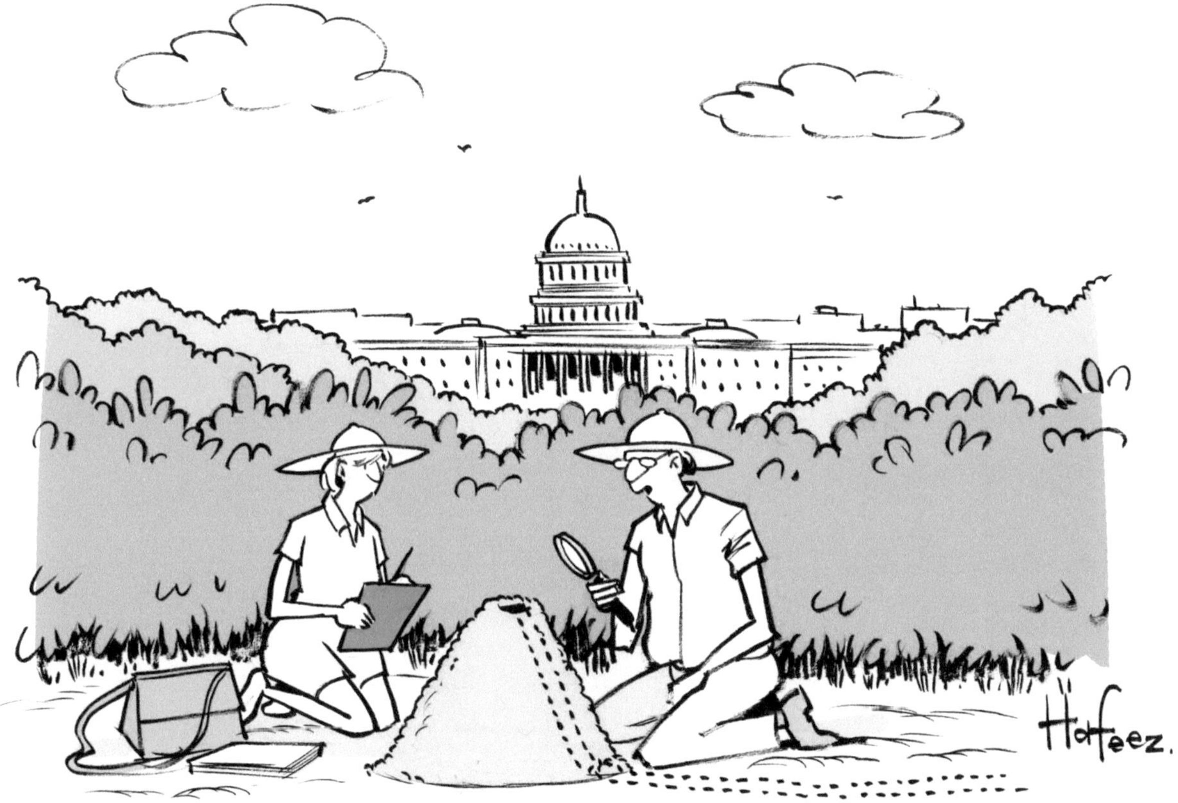
Hafeez.

"It always amazes me how extremely simple creatures, with no capacity for communication, can achieve the appearance of joint decision-making."

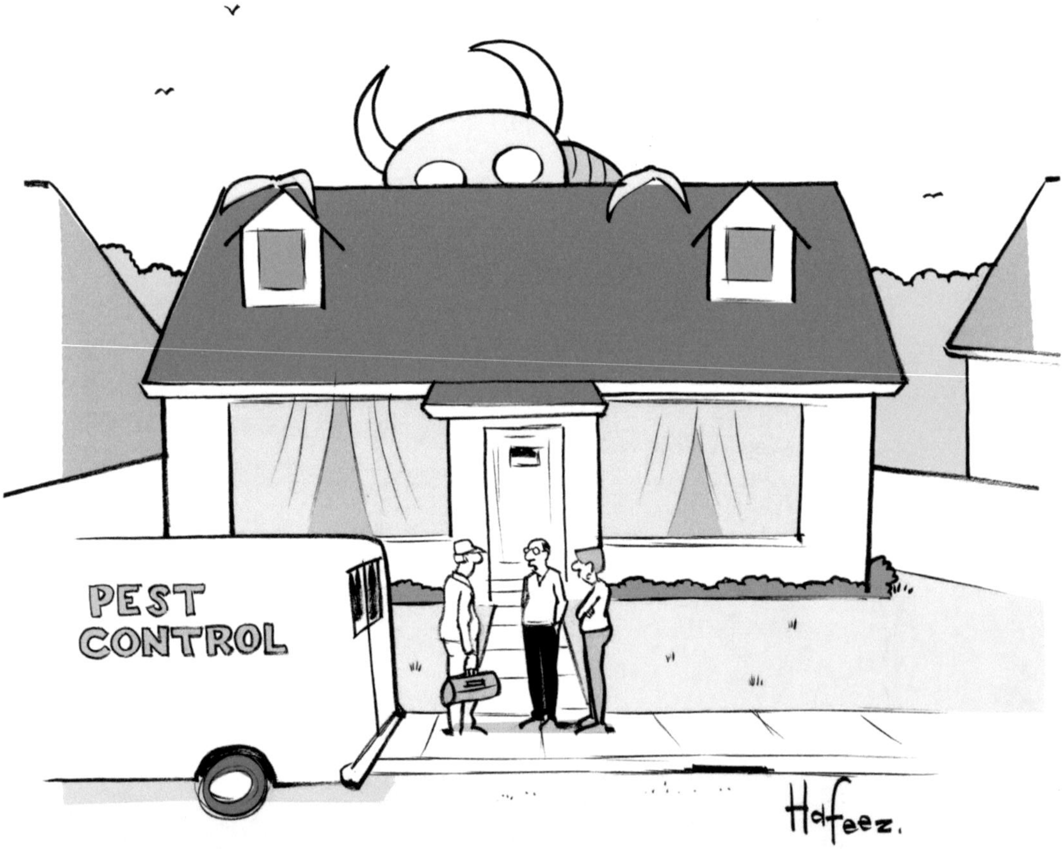
PEST
CONTROL
Hafeez.

"We have a termite problem."

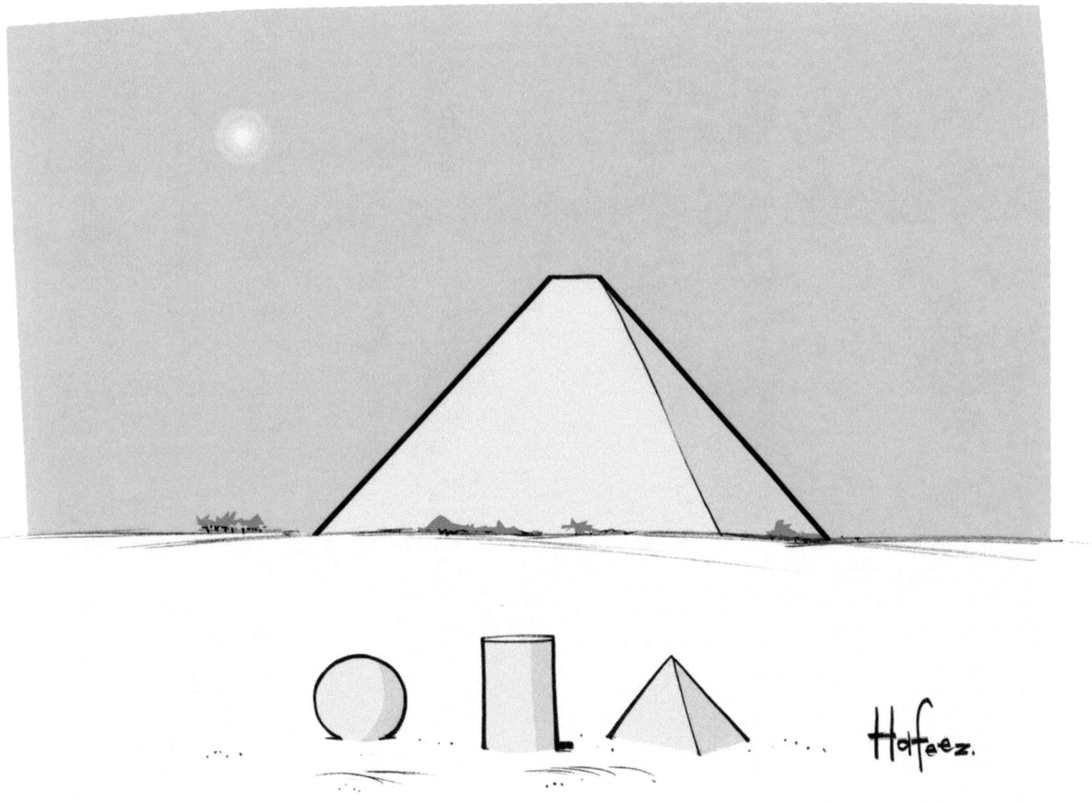
Hafeez.

THE FINALISTS FOR GIZA'S CAPSTONE CONTEST

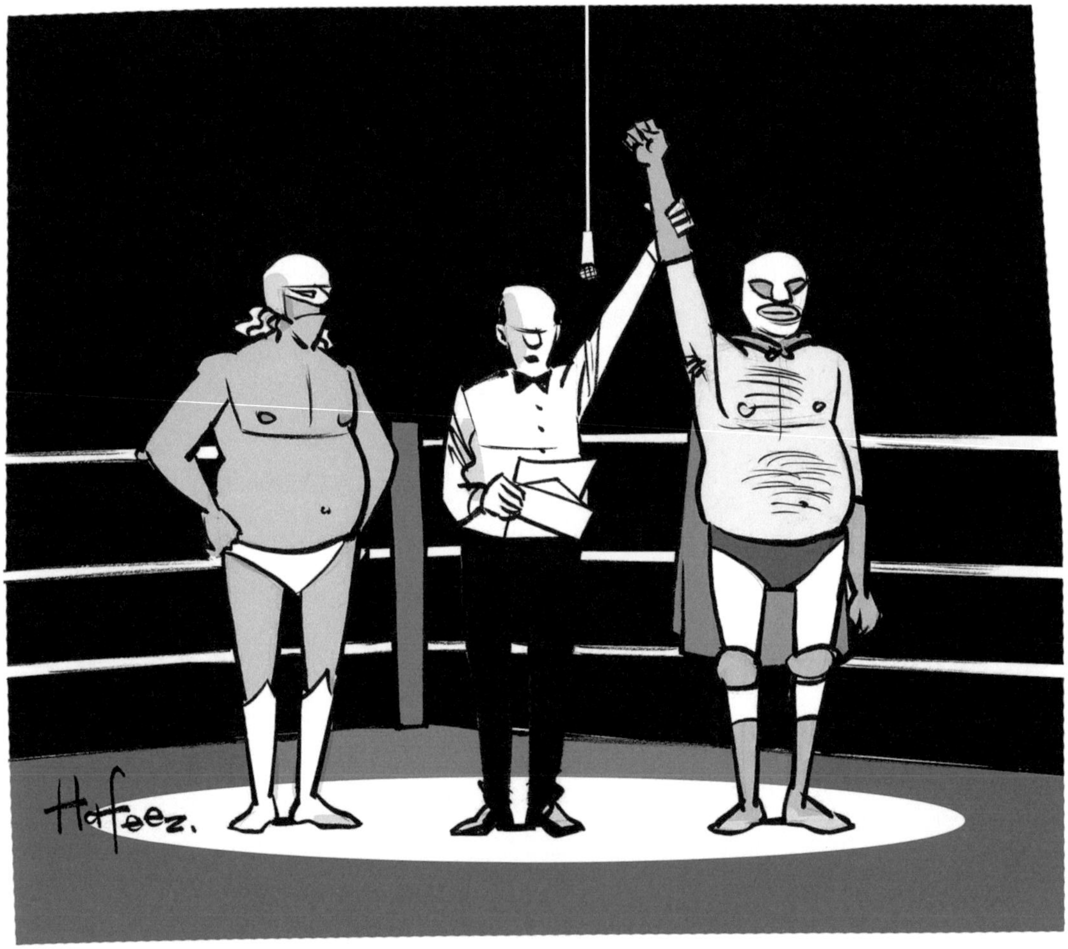
Hafeez.

“... and the awards for Best Actor in a Leading Role, Best Costume Design, and Best Stunt Coordination ...... The Anvil!”

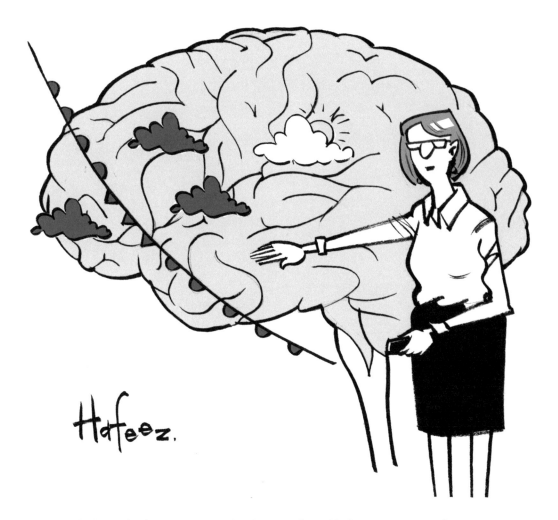

"Today's forecast calls for heavy fog all day, with brief periods of clarity mid-afternoon, followed by a seasonal depression later this evening as dark clouds gather on the horizon ."

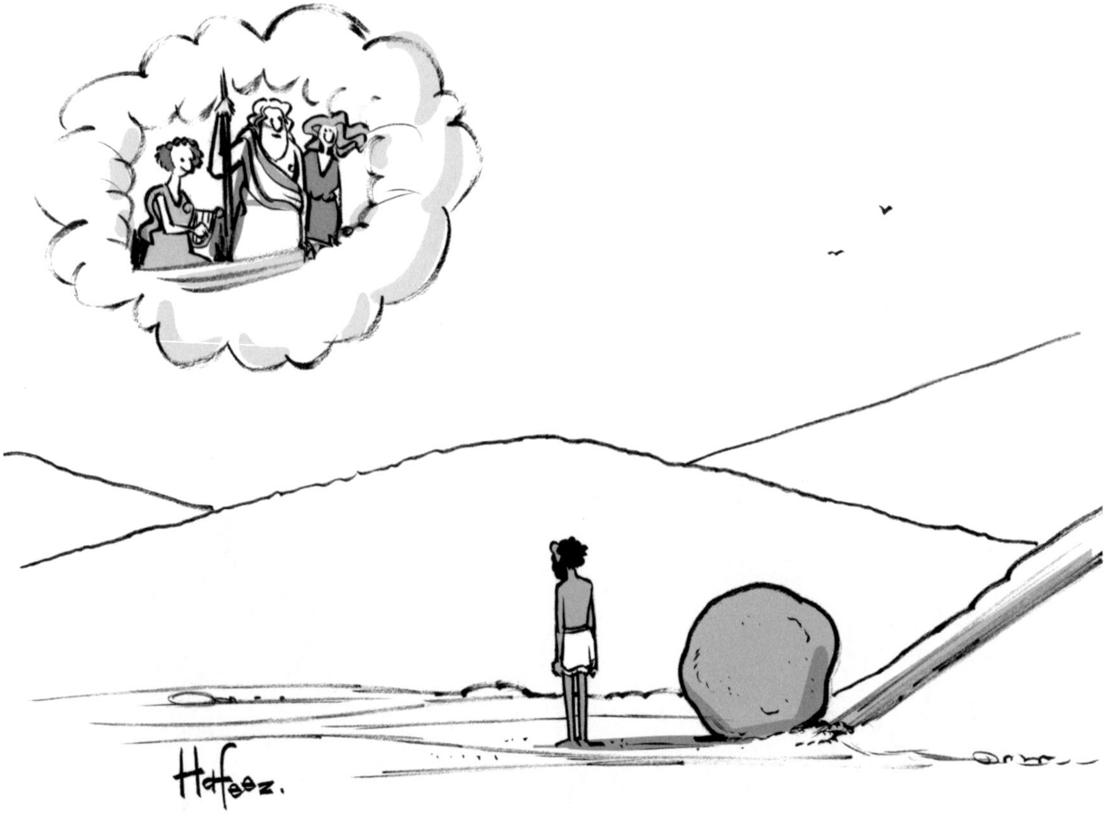
Hafeez.

"We've decided to change your punishment. From now on, you will purchase a lottery ticket every week, only to have your hopes come crashing down each time you inevitably lose."

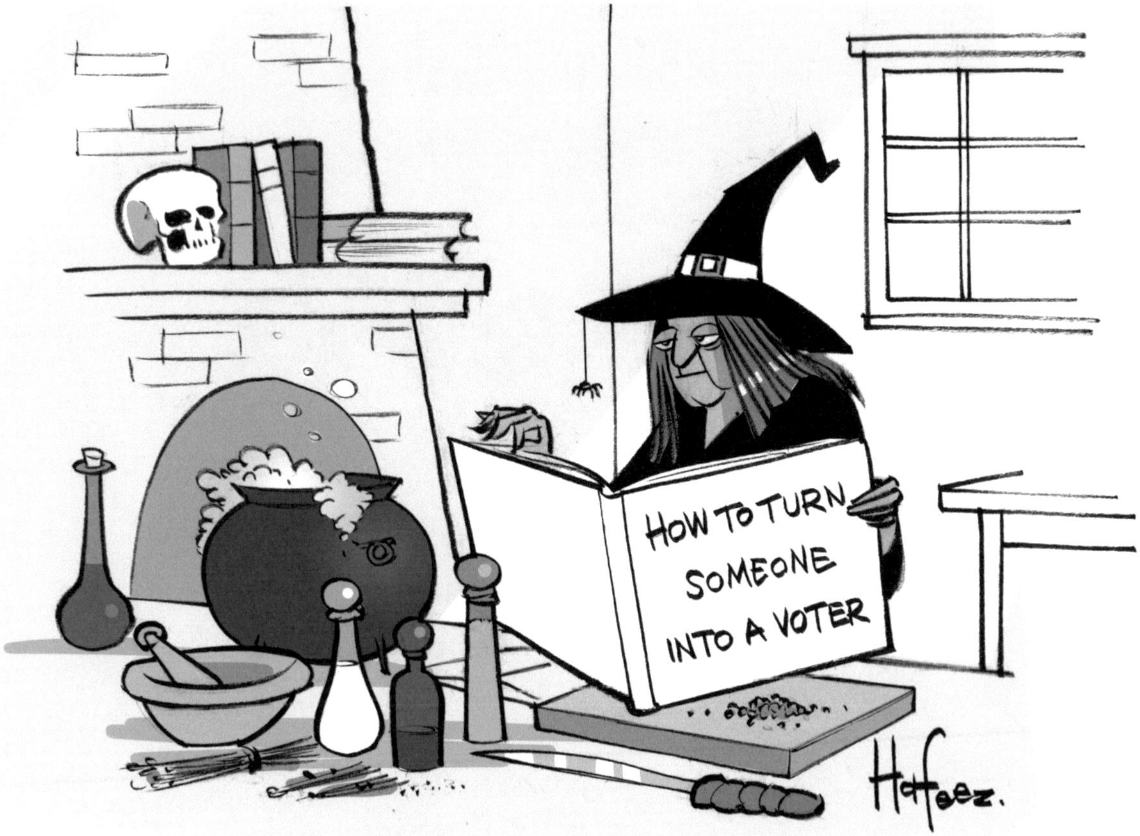
HOW TO TURN SOMEONE INTO A VOTER
Hafeez.

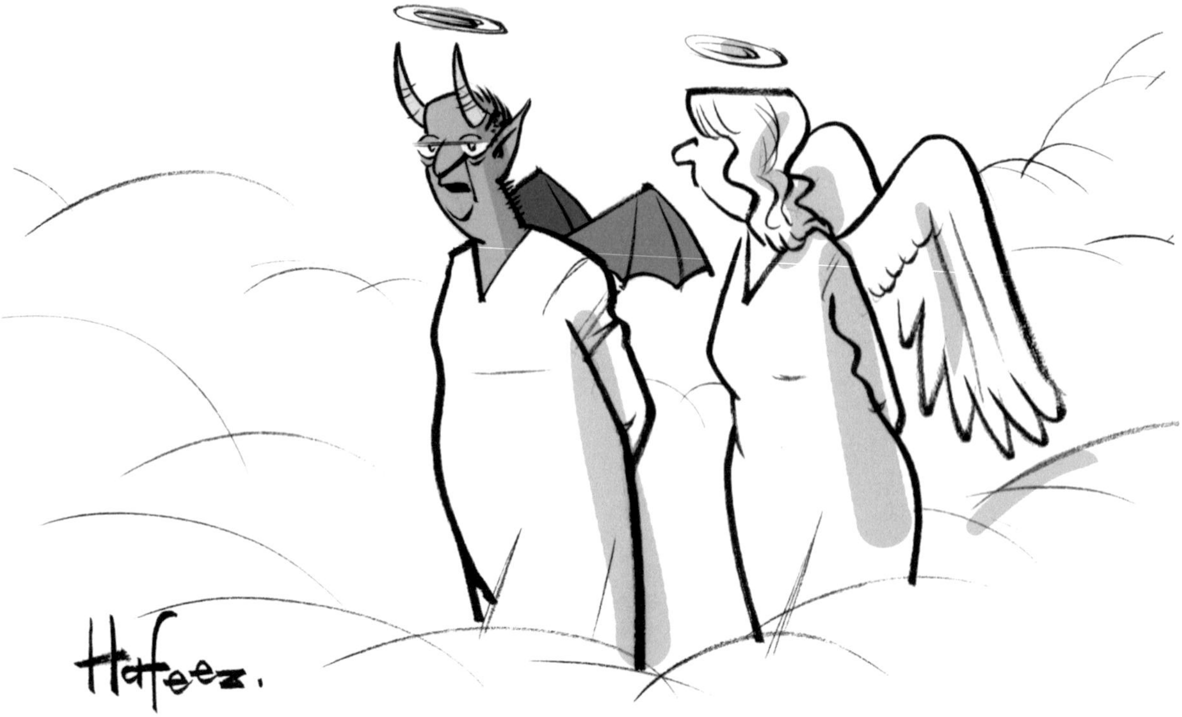
Hafeez.

"I was lucky—my parents went to Heaven."

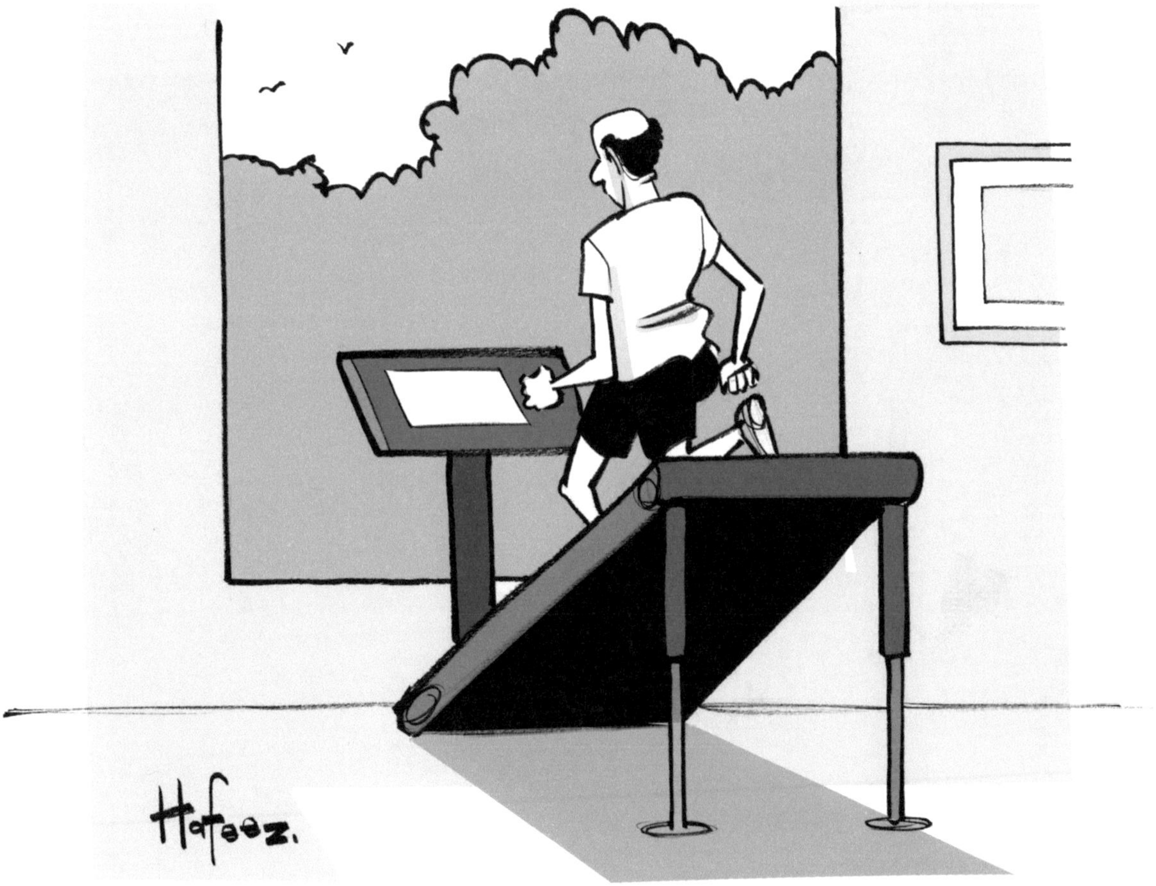
Hafeez.

THE OVER-40 WORKOUT

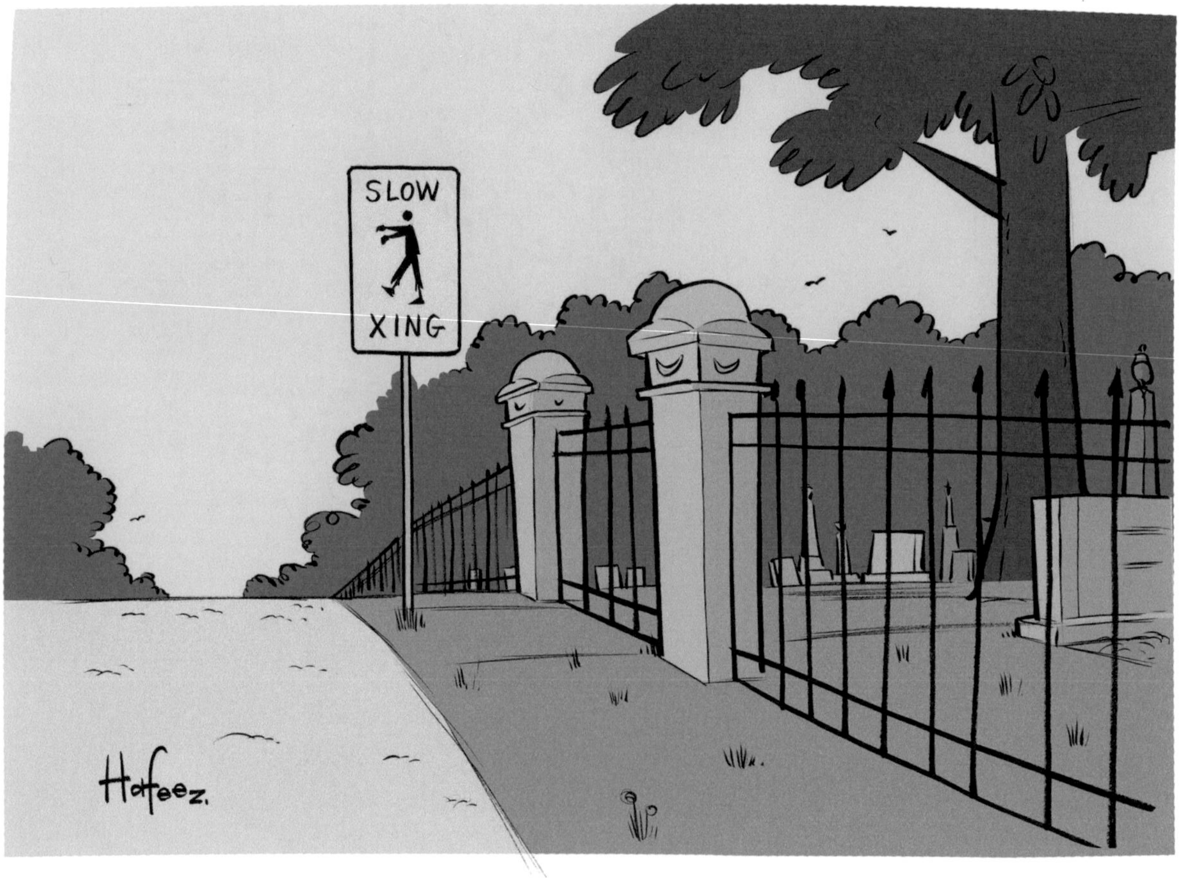
SLOW
XING
Hafeez.

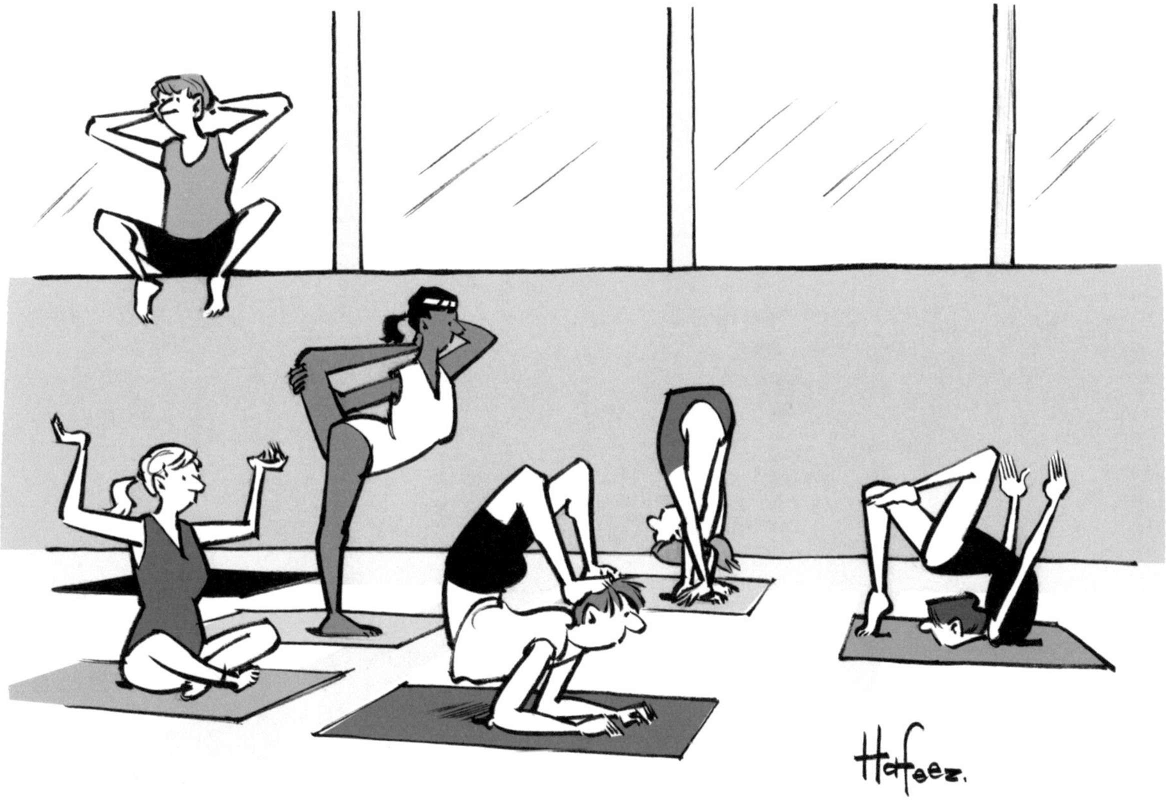
Hafeez.

IMPROV YOGA CLASS

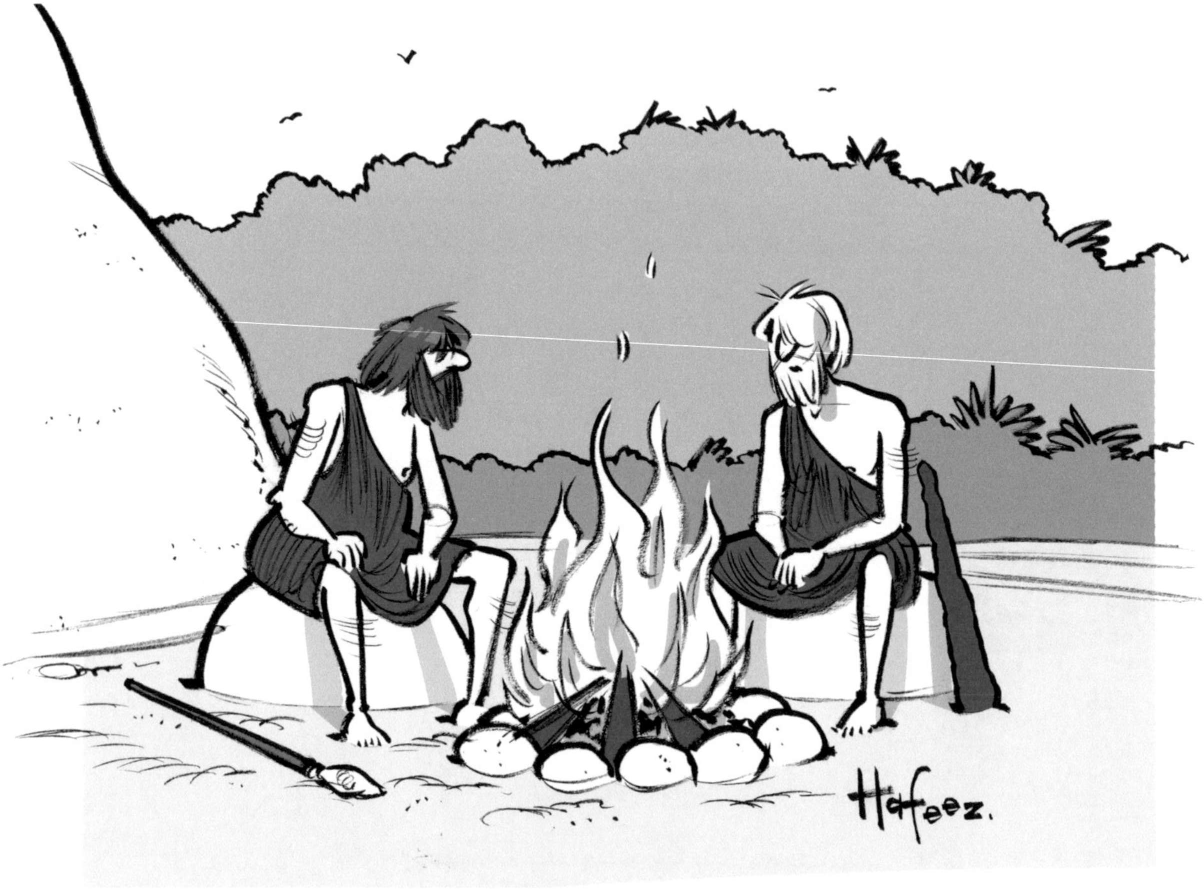
Hafeez.

"I don't know about you, but ever since we invented language I've been getting a lot less sex."

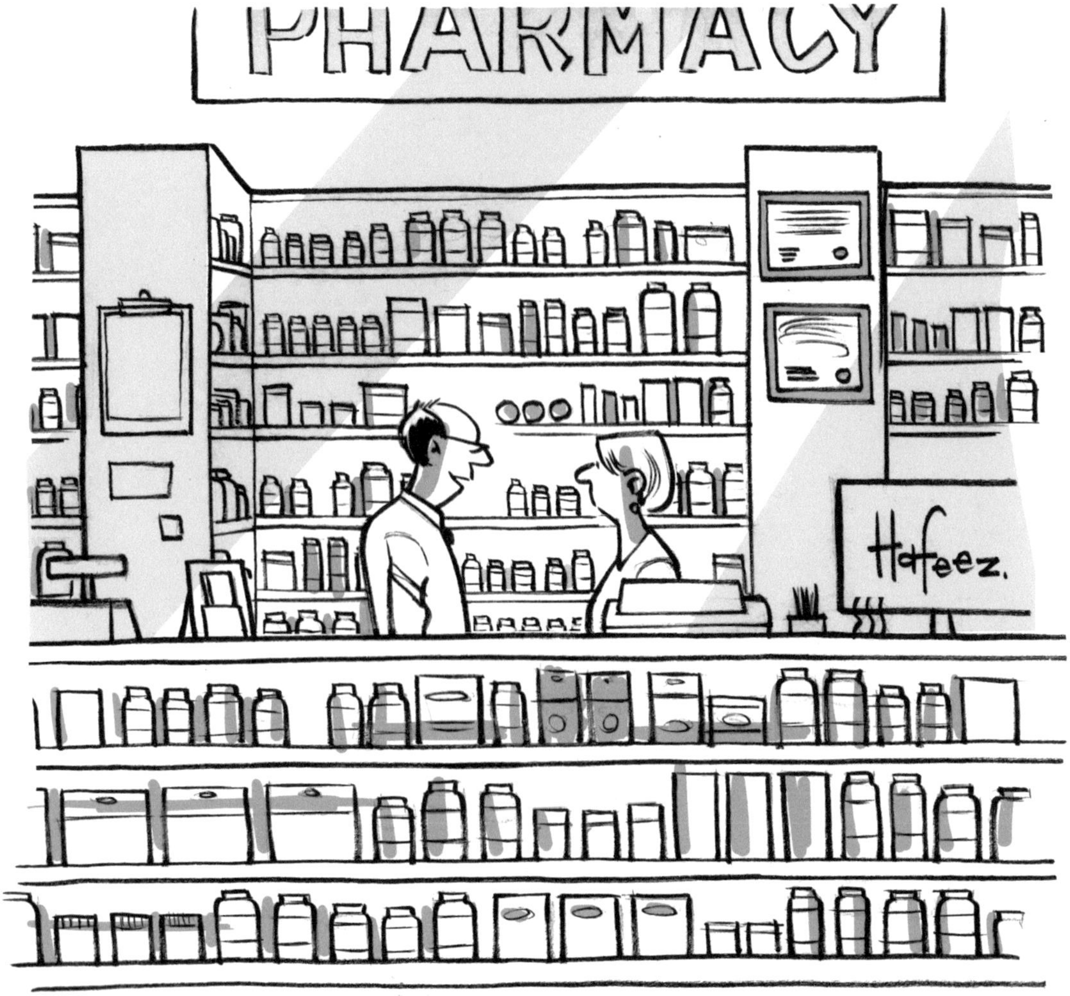
PHARMACY
Hafeez.

"I'll let you in on a little secret of mine—every pill on these shelves is a placebo, and I've never been to pharmacy school."

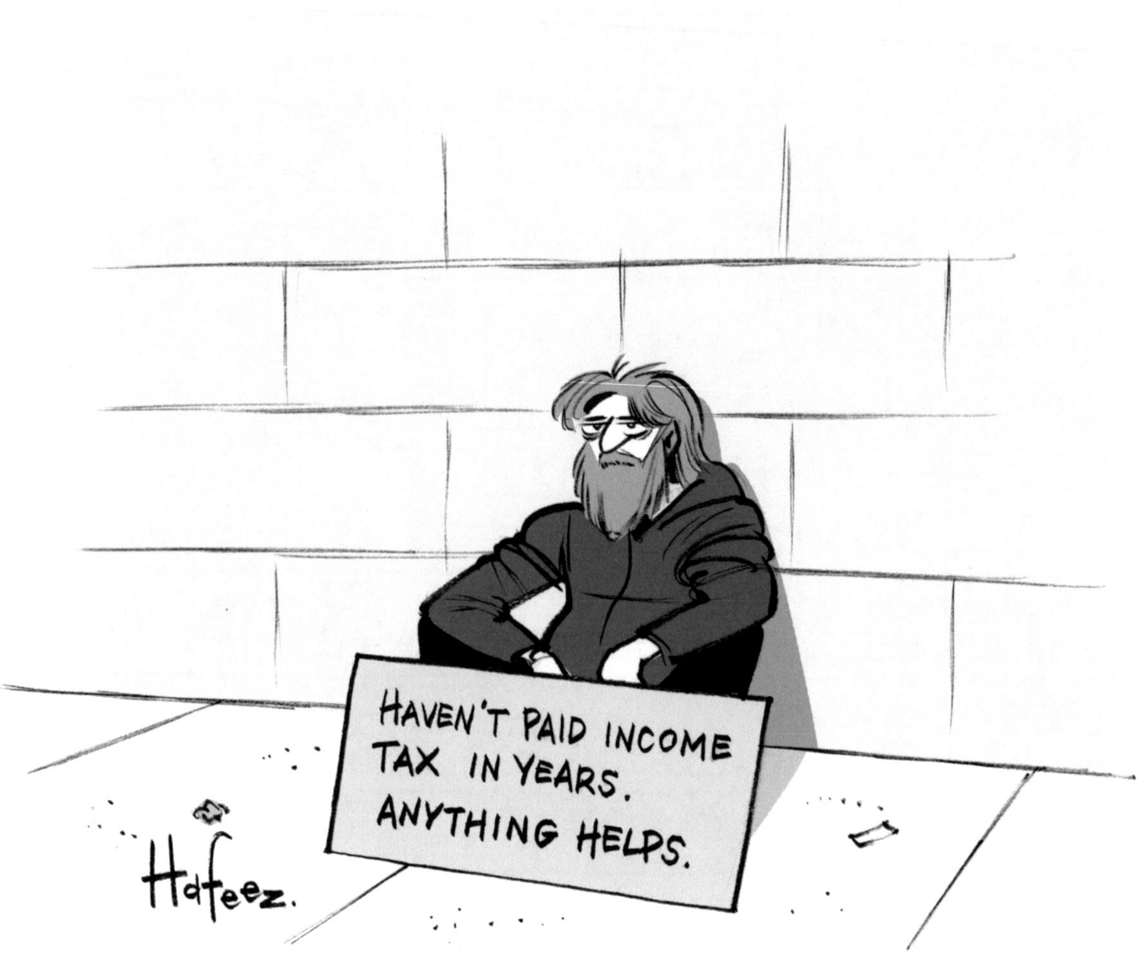
HAVEN'T PAID INCOME
TAX IN YEARS.
ANYTHING HELPS.
Hafeez.

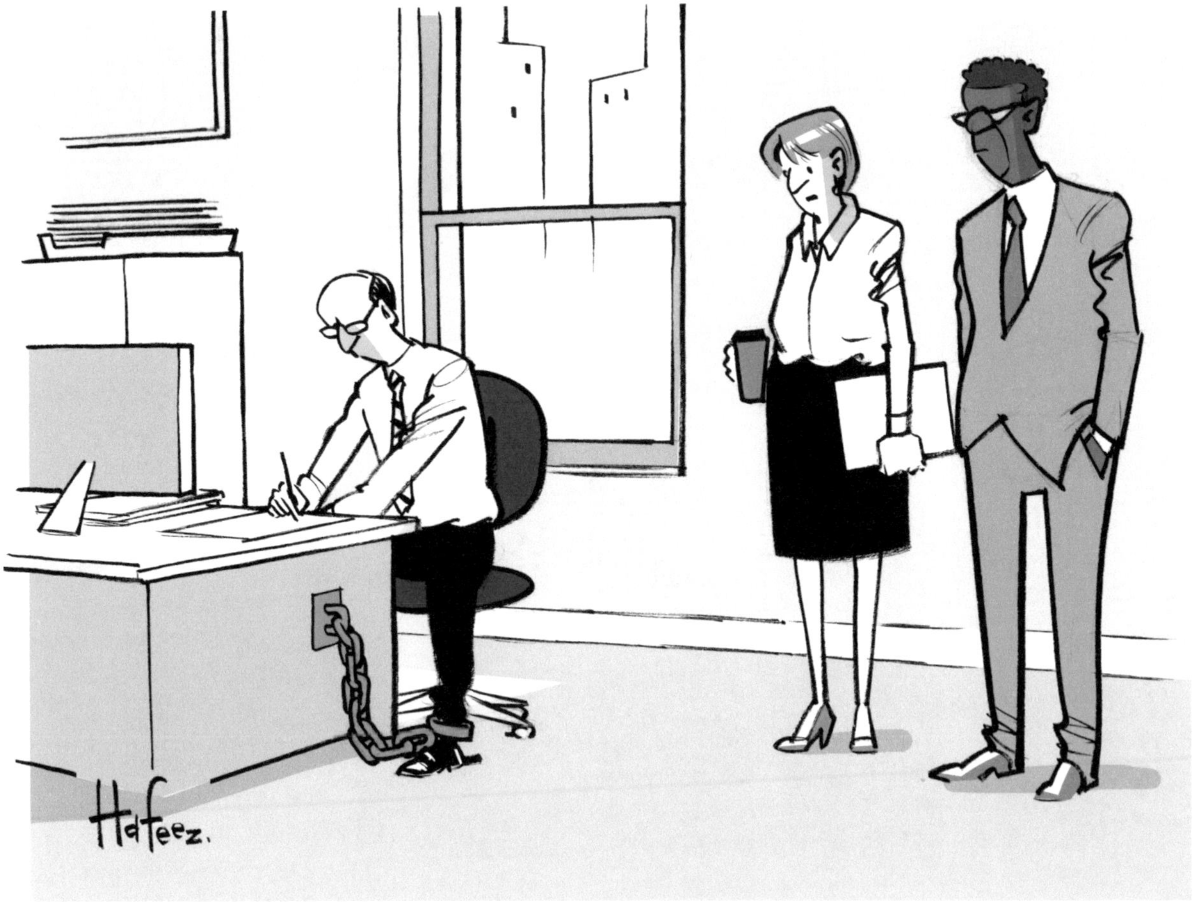
Hafeez.

"That must be the new 'sit-work' desk."

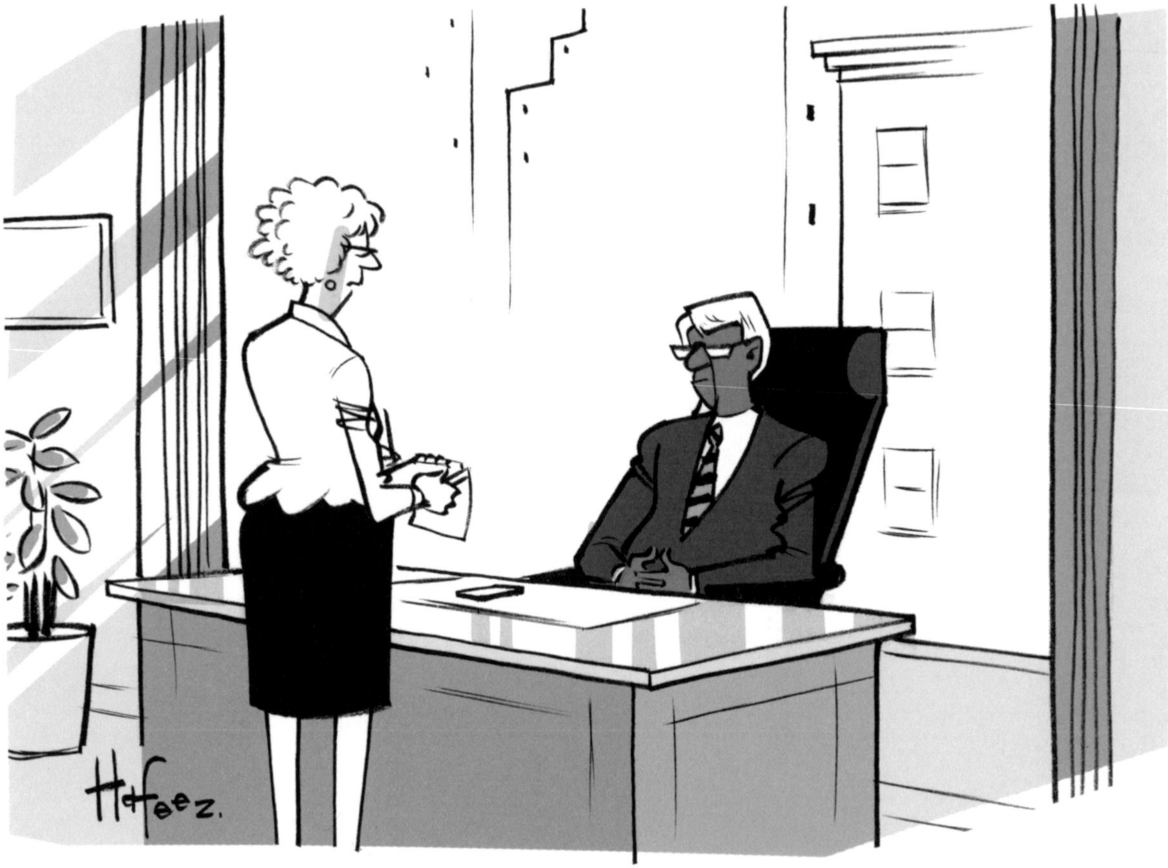
Hafeez.

"Also, your wife called to remind you today is the tenth anniversary of your bailout."

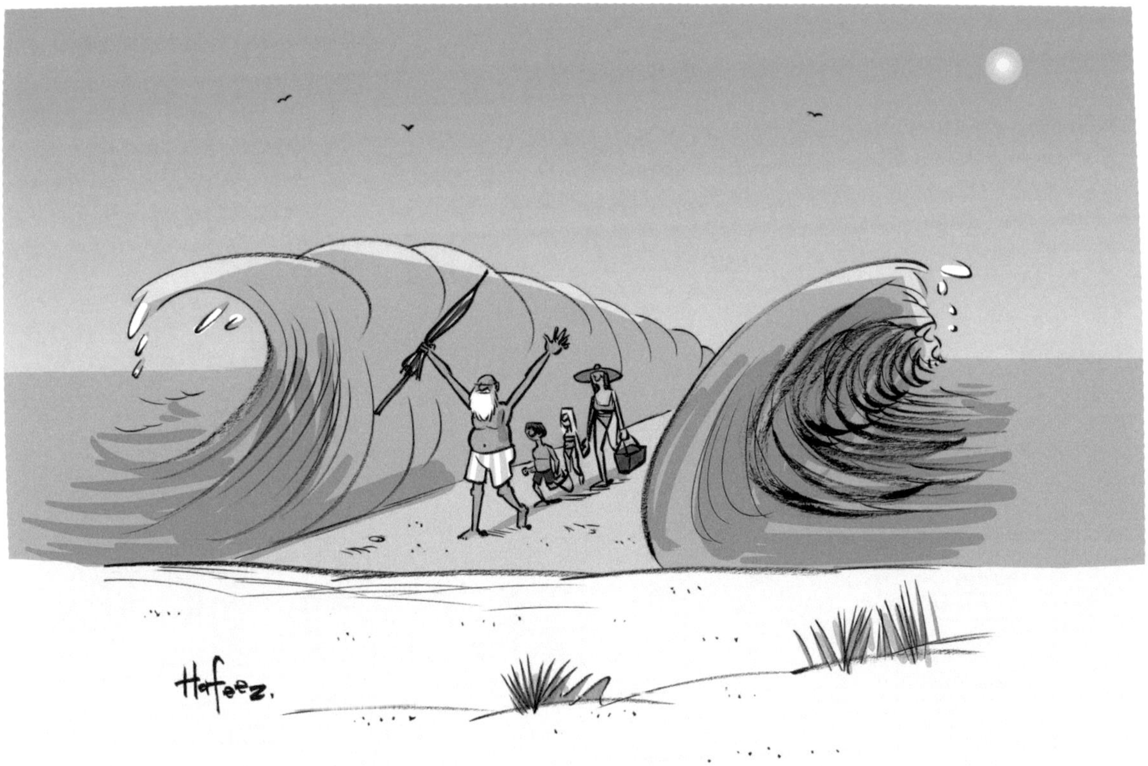
Hafeez.

MOSES PARTS MAIN BEACH

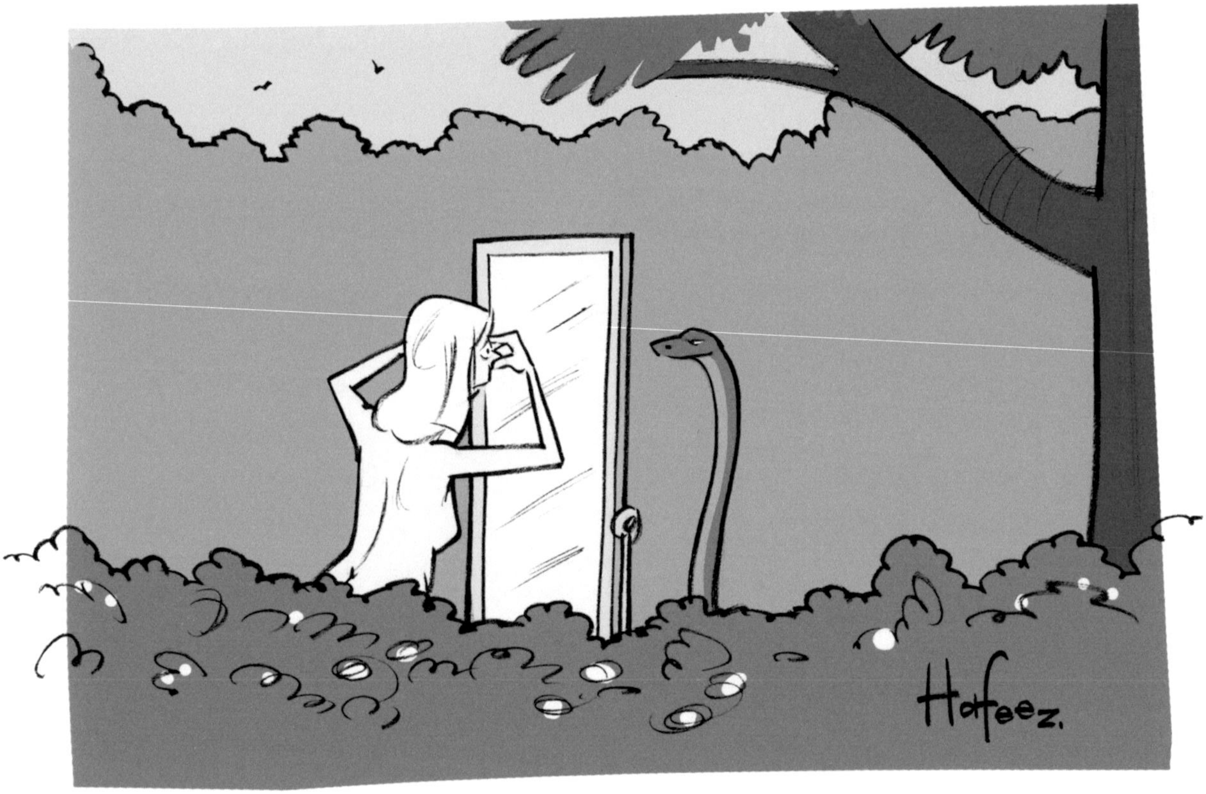
Hafeez.

"I didn't know my eyebrows looked like that."

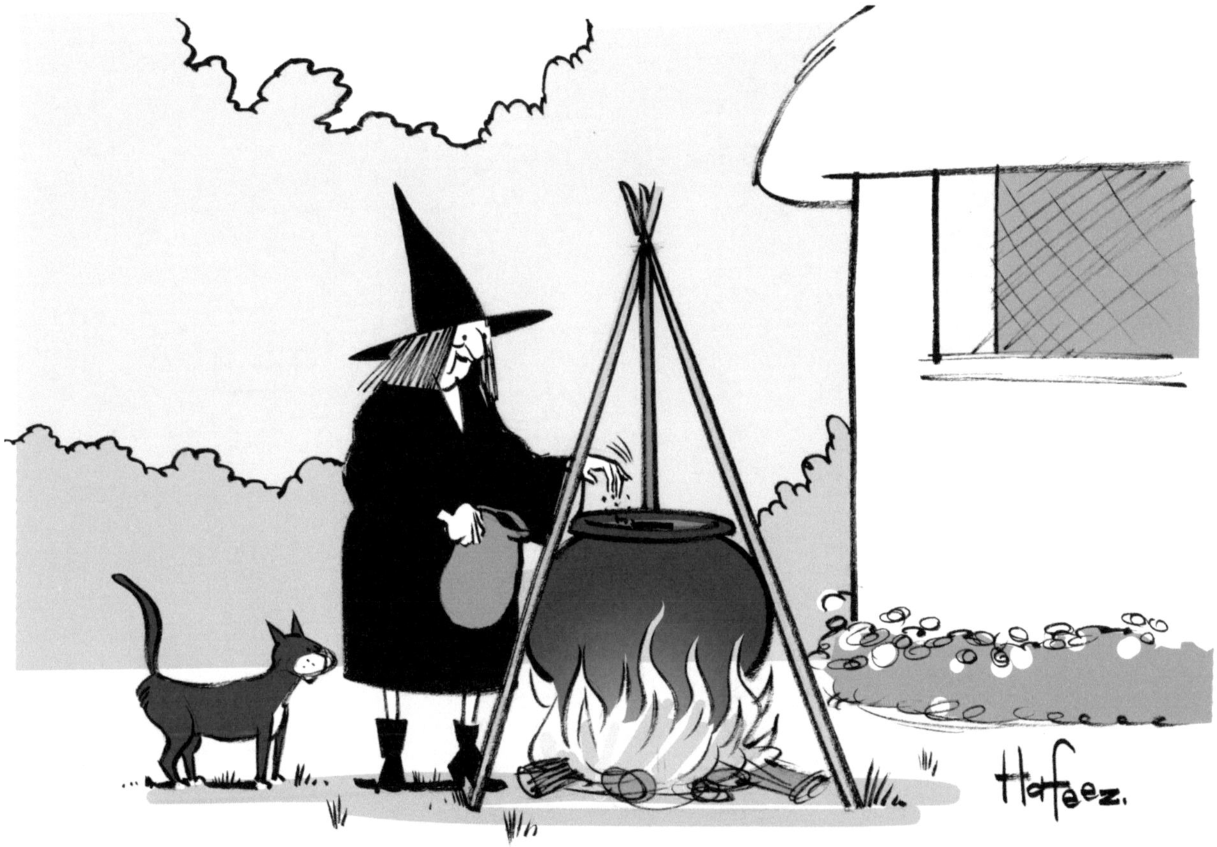
Hafeez.

"Round about the cauldron we go, in the exfoliating toner I throw."

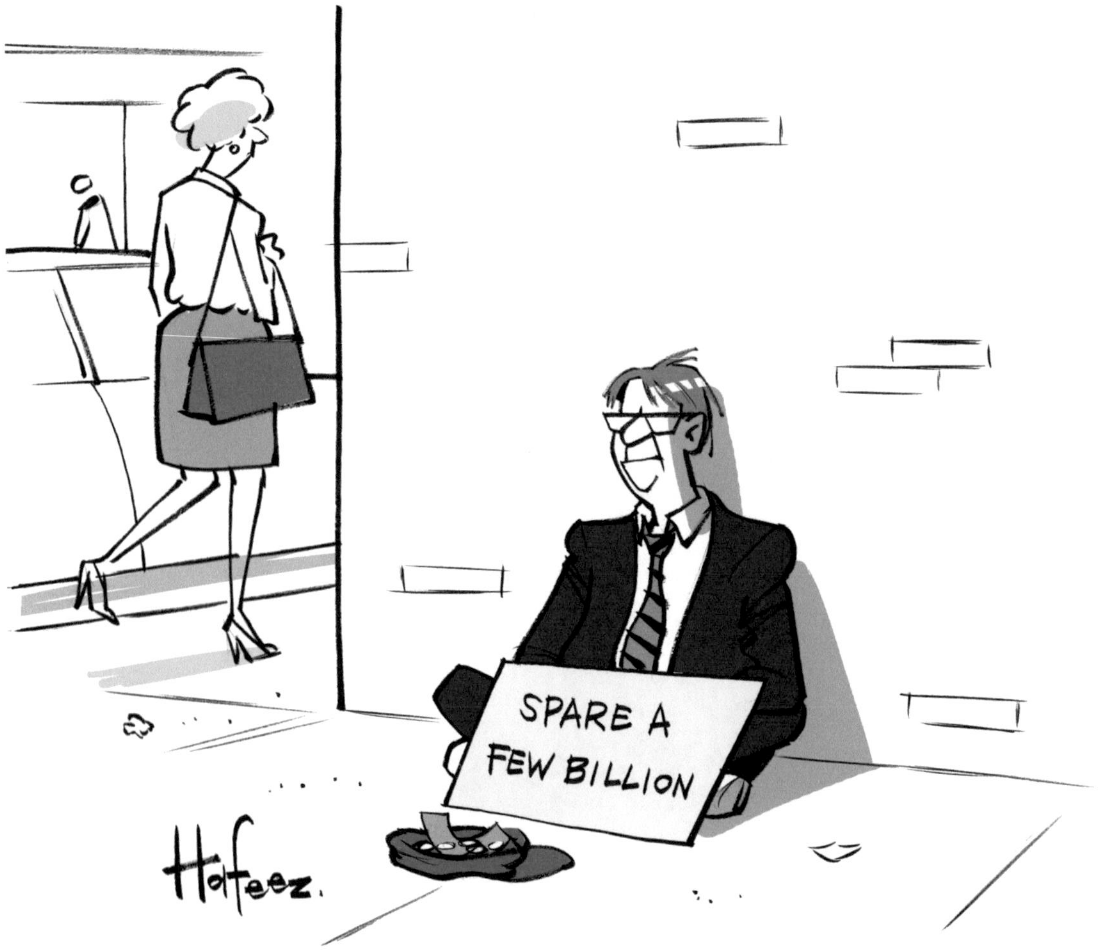
SPARE A
FEW BILLION
Hafeez.

Kaamran Hafeez has been writing, drawing, and selling cartoons to the magazine markets since 2010. Prior to that, he drew a digitally syndicated panel for GoComics called, "Bozo". Kaamran's cartoons have appeared in *The New Yorker, Barron's, The Wall Street Journal, Reader's Digest, Saturday Evening Post,* and *Harvard Business Review.*

Kaamran lives and works on Gabriola Island, B.C., where he runs the local chess club.

Printed in the United States
By Bookmasters